Knowledge Management for Sales and Marketing

CHANDOS
KNOWLEDGE MANAGEMENT SERIES

Chandos' new series of books is aimed at all those individuals interested in Knowledge Management. They have been specially commissioned to provide the reader with an authoritative view of current thinking. If you would like a full listing of current and forthcoming titles, please visit our website www. chandospublishing.com or e-mail info@chandospublishing.com or telephone +44 (0) 1223 499140.

New authors: we are always pleased to receive ideas for new titles; if you would like to write a book for Chandos, please contact Dr Glyn Jones on e-mail gjones@ chandospublishing.com or telephone number +44 (0) 1993 848726.

Bulk orders: some organisations buy a number of copies of our books. If you are interested in doing this, we would be pleased to discuss a discount. Please e-mail info@chandospublishing.com or telephone +44 (0) 1223 499140.

Knowledge Management for Sales and Marketing

A practitioner's guide

TOM YOUNG AND NICK MILTON

Oxford Cambridge New Delhi

Chandos Publishing
TBAC Business Centre
Avenue 4
Station Lane
Witney
Oxford OX28 4BN
UK
Tel: +44 (0) 1993 848726
Email: info@chandospublishing.com
www.chandospublishing.com

Chandos Publishing is an imprint of Woodhead Publishing Limited

Woodhead Publishing Limited
80 High Street
Sawston
Cambridge CB22 3HJ
UK
www.woodheadpublishing.com

First published in 2011

ISBN:
978 1 84334 604 3
(Chandos Publishing)

British Library Cataloguing-in-Publication Data.
A catalogue record for this book is available from the British Library.

Typeset by RefineCatch Limited, Bungay, Suffolk
Printed in the UK and USA.

Contents

List of figures and table

Figures

Table

Foreword

The breadth and depth of knowledge that the management consultancy Knoco have in the field of knowledge management is without equal. For that reason the publisher commissioned them to publish a series of books looking at how knowledge management is applied in different circumstances. These books have become standard texts within the profession so when Tom approached me to discuss some of his ideas for a book targeted on knowledge management in sales and marketing I was delighted. I have known Tom for many years and collaborated on several business ventures with him and found his ability to relate to people of differing backgrounds, seniority and disciplines to be of immense value to our business.

This book looks at the end-to-end cycle of sales and sales management and is relevant to all aspects of selling, whether it is large complex solution sales or simple one-off customer engagements.

The book will be of value to the knowledge management practitioner looking for guidance on how to introduce knowledge management to the sales and marketing activities of their company. In addition it will provide real value to sales and marketing people seeking to improve their own individual performance through managing knowledge.

The years of experience of practical implementation of knowledge management shine out of the pages of this book. This is not a dry, academic book but a must-read for everyone involved in knowledge management, sales or marketing.

Colin Mattey
Former Sales Director, BT Commercial and Brands and currently MD, Steria UK, Commercial Sector

Preface

This book is part of the Chandos Knowledge Management series. It deals with knowledge management as applied within a sales and marketing environment. There is an inevitable overlap in content with the previous titles, *Knowledge Management for Teams and Projects* and *Knowledge Management for Services, Operations and Manufacturing*.

This book is written primarily for the knowledge management practitioner looking for guidance on how to establish a knowledge management system for their sales and marketing departments. Hopefully it will also be useful to managers of sales and marketing departments as they seek to improve the efficiency and effectiveness of their departments. Lastly, it will be of use to individuals working in sales and marketing as they seek to improve their own performance.

Based on the experience of successful and unsuccessful knowledge management systems the book recognises the need to convert knowledge and learning into action. For this to happen, there needs to be a framework of processes, technologies, roles and governance in place, and the authors aim to guide the reader through these elements. If all elements are present and operating well, knowledge management can give huge performance benefits to an organisation. However, failure to implement the entire system can result in the flow of knowledge being blocked, corrupted or diverted at any stage, and little or no value will then be delivered.

The aim of this book is to provide practical guidelines to managing knowledge within a sales and marketing environment, illustrated with case histories from the authors, contributors and industry.

Acknowledgements

We would like to acknowledge the input provided to this book by Colin Mattey, for his insights into managing sales and marketing professionals; John Davies, Ian Thurlow and Paul Warren, who wrote Chapter 8; Linda Davies, who wrote Chapter 9; Graeme Smith, who contributed Chapter 10; and Ankey Heley, who used her extensive experience in the sales and marketing field when proofreading the text.

Tom and Nick would like to thank their wives and families for their support and tolerance during the writing of this book.

About the authors

Tom Young and Dr Nick Milton are directors and founders of Knoco Ltd – a knowledge management consultancy comprising seasoned knowledge management practitioners, mentors and coaches. Knoco Ltd has been delivering successful and sustained knowledge management implementation to clients since 1999.

Tom is one of the leading practitioners of knowledge management. An engineer by training, Tom has worked in a number of industries and in many countries around the world. This unique breadth and depth of understanding of the business world, supplemented with MBA training, allows him to understand the challenges being faced by CEOs and the wider workforce. He then works with them to craft solutions that deliver sustainable business benefits. Tom was the driving force behind BP's Knowledge Management Team, working with business units around the world to understand what knowledge management meant in their context and how to implement KM within their environment. His work with retail set the standard for what can be achieved in KM.

Tom is in constant demand as a KM consultant and has led many of Knoco's largest projects. His role as Knoco chairman ensures that this experience of practical knowledge management is shared with the growing family of Knoco franchise companies. He is the author of *Knowledge Management for Services, Operations and Manufacturing*. He is also a past president of the Chamber of Commerce.

Before joining Knoco Ltd, Nick was a core member of the BP Knowledge Management Team, developing and implementing BP's knowledge of 'how to manage knowledge', and coordinating the BP Knowledge Management Community of Practice. Prior to this role he worked for five years as Knowledge Manager for BP Norway, starting this role in 1992. In this role he created and operated a lessons learned system for the business unit, which coincided with one of its most successful exploration periods.

As a consultant for Knoco, Nick has facilitated knowledge management activities and strategies for major organisations around the world. He is the author of *The Lessons Learned Handbook* and *Knowledge Management for Teams and Projects*, and co-author of *Performance Through Learning – Knowledge Management in Practice*.

Principles of knowledge management

Introduction

It is traditional to start a book of this type with the discussion of 'what is knowledge'?, and 'what is knowledge management'?. If you are already quite clear about the topic, then this chapter is not for you. However, there is often still some confusion over the definitions of, and fuzzy boundaries between, knowledge management, information management and data management. The two latter disciplines are well established; people know what they mean, people are trained in them, there are plenty of reference books that explain what they are and how they work. *Knowledge management*, on the other hand, is a relatively new term and one that requires a little bit of explanation. If you would rather jump on to the practical applications, start at Chapter 2 and come back to Chapter 1 another day.

The greater part of Chapter 1 necessarily covers much of the same ground as the corresponding sections in Milton (2004)[1] and in Young (2009).[2] If you own and have read these two books, you can move on to Chapter 2.

We will start by looking at 'what is knowledge?'

What is knowledge?

Knowledge (according to Peter Senge[3]) is 'the ability to take effective action' (the Singapore Armed Forces further refine this definition as 'the capacity to take effective action in varied and uncertain situations'). Knowledge is something that only humans can possess. People know things and can act on them; computers can't know things and can only respond. This ability to take effective action is based on experience and it involves the application of theory or heuristics (rules of thumb) to situations – either consciously or unconsciously. Knowledge has

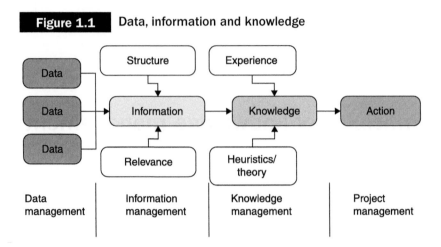

Figure 1.1 Data, information and knowledge

something that data and information lack, and those extra ingredients are the experience and the heuristics (Figure 1.1).

Knowledge is situational and what works in one situation may not work in another.

As an illustration, consider the link between data, information and knowledge as they are involved in decision-making in a marketing organisation:

- The company pays for a market research survey, conducting interviews with a selection of consumers in several market segments. Each interview is a datapoint. These data are held in a database of survey responses.

- In order for these data to be interpreted, they need to be presented in a meaningful way. The market research company analyses the data and pulls out trends and statistics that they present as charts, graphs and analyses.

- However, you need to know what to do with this information. You need to know what action to take as a result. Such information, even presented in statistics and graphs, is meaningless to the layman, but an experienced marketer can look at it, consider the business context and the current situation, apply their experience, use some theory, heuristics or rules of thumb, and can make a decision about the future marketing approach. That decision may be to conduct some further sampling, to launch a new campaign, or to rerun an existing campaign.

The experienced marketer has 'know-how' – he or she knows how to interpret market research information. They can use that knowledge to take the information and decide on an effective action. Their know-how is developed from training, from years of experience, through the acquisition of a set of heuristics and working models, and through many conference and bar-room conversations with the wider community of marketers.

Knowledge that leads to action is 'know-how'. Your experience, and the theories and heuristics to which you have access, allow you to know what to do, and to know how to do it. In this book, you can use the terms 'knowledge' and 'know-how' interchangeably.

In large organisations, and in organisations where people work in teams and networks, knowledge and know-how are increasingly being seen as a communal possession, rather than an individual possession. In some companies it will be the communities of practice that have the collective ownership of the knowledge, while in others it will be the regional sales teams that have the collective ownership. Such knowledge is 'common knowledge' – the things that everybody knows. This common knowledge is based on shared experiences and on collective theory and heuristics that are defined, agreed and validated by the community.

Tacit and explicit knowledge

The terms *tacit* and *explicit* are often used when talking about knowledge. The original author, Polyani (1966),[4] used these terms to define 'unable to be expressed' and 'able to be expressed' respectively. Thus, in the original usage, tacit knowledge means knowledge held instinctively, in the unconscious mind and in the muscle memory, which cannot be transferred into words. Knowledge of how to ride a bicycle, for example, is tacit knowledge, as it is almost impossible to explain verbally.

Following the seminal text by Nonaka and Takeuchi (1995)[5] these original definitions have become blurred, and tacit and explicit are often used to describe 'knowledge which has not been codified' and 'knowledge which has been codified' (or 'head knowledge' and 'recorded knowledge' respectively). This latter definition is a more useful one in the context of knowledge management within organisations, as it defines knowledge based on where it exists, rather than on its intrinsic codifiability. So, knowledge that exists only in people's heads is often termed *tacit knowledge*, and knowledge that has been recorded somewhere is termed *explicit knowledge*. Knowledge can therefore be transferred from tacit to explicit, according to Nonaka and Takeuchi.

There is a wide range of types of knowledge, from easily codifiable to completely uncodifiable. Some know-how, such as how to cook a pizza, can be codified and written down; indeed, most households contain codified cooking knowledge (cookery books). Other know-how, such as how to whistle or how to dance the tango, cannot be codified, and there would be no point in trying to teach someone to dance by giving them a book on the subject.

Sales and marketing knowledge comprises a wide range of codifiability. Some of it can never be fully written down, e.g. how to establish a lasting relationship with a client, and must be transferred through coaching and role-play, while some of it can be easily codified into company guidelines.

What is knowledge management?

If knowledge is a combination of experience, theory and heuristics, developed by an individual or a community of practice, that allows decisions to be made and correct actions to be taken, then what is knowledge management? Larry Prusak of McKinsey Consulting says, 'It is the attempt to recognise what is essentially a human asset buried in the minds of individuals, and leverage it into a corporate asset that can be used by a broader set of individuals, on whose decisions the firm depends' (Prusak, verbal communication). Larry is suggesting here that the shift from seeing knowledge as personal property to seeing knowledge as communal property is at the heart of knowledge management (leveraging the personal to help a broader set of individuals). To ensure that knowledge management is a true management discipline, we need to make sure that this is done systematically, routinely and in service of business strategy.

Our preferred definition, however, is that 'knowledge management is the way you manage your team or your organisation, with due attention to the value of knowledge'. Knowledge management is therefore a managerial response to recognising the value of an asset. The managerial response – the processes, accountabilities and technologies applied – will vary depending on your organisational context. The unifying factor between these approaches is their focus on delivering value through knowledge, by making sure that people who need to take action have (or have access to) the knowledge to make that action effective.

Given that knowledge is intangible, knowledge management is not easy. However, modern businesses are becoming increasingly familiar with the practice of managing intangibles. Risk management, customer relations management, safety management and brand management are all recognised management approaches. Knowledge is not significantly less tangible or less measurable than risk, brand, reputation or safety, and the term 'management' suggests a healthy level of rigour and business focus. The value of a brand is enormous, and therefore brands need to be managed. The value of corporate knowledge is also enormous, so why should that value not also be managed? Brand, reputation, knowledge, customer base, etc., are intangible assets with great value to the organisation, and to leave these assets unmanaged would seem to be foolish in the extreme.

There is, in the literature and in current (2010) practice, much confusion between knowledge management and information management. You will find many definitions of knowledge management that refer only to information (for example the popular 'knowledge management means getting the right information to the right people at the right time') or to explicit content. In these cases, you could replace 'knowledge management' with 'information management' or 'content management' and the definition would still be valid. Knowledge management is more than information management and more than content management, and involves more than the provision of information or explicit content. Knowledge management needs to address the tacit as well as the explicit. It needs to cover access to experience and judgement as well as access to information.

Knowledge management models

In this section we look at some simple models for the management of knowledge and at some of the enabling factors that need to be in place to support these models. Some of the ideas and models introduced here will be built upon throughout the rest of the book.

Knowledge suppliers and users

Prusak's definition presented in the previous section implies the existence of suppliers of knowledge ('individuals') and users of knowledge ('others'), people in whose minds the knowledge is buried and people and teams who need access to that knowledge.

Knowledge is created through experience and through the reflection on experience in order to derive guidelines, rules, theories, heuristics and doctrines. Knowledge may be created by individuals, through reflecting on their own experience, or it may be created by teams reflecting on team experience. It may also be created by experts or communities of practice reflecting on the experience of many individuals and teams across an organisation. The individuals, teams and communities who do this reflecting can be considered as 'knowledge suppliers'.

In business activity, knowledge is applied by individuals and teams. They can apply their own personal knowledge and experience, or they can look elsewhere for knowledge – to learn before they start, by seeking the knowledge of others. The more knowledgeable they are at the start of the activity or project, the more likely they are to avoid mistakes, repeat good practice, and avoid risk. These people are 'knowledge users'.

We have introduced the idea of tacit knowledge and explicit knowledge. The knowledge can be transferred from the supplier to the user tacitly, through dialogue, or explicitly, through codifying the knowledge. Figure 1.2 shows these two approaches by looking at the two places where knowledge can be stored: in people's heads or in codified form in some sort of 'knowledge bank' (Figure 1.2 is a redrafting of the SECI model of Nonaka and Takeuchi). These two stores can be connected in four ways:

- direct transfer of knowledge from person to person (communication);
- transfer of knowledge from people to the 'knowledge bank' (knowledge capture);
- organisation of knowledge within the knowledge bank (organisation);
- transfer of knowledge from the 'knowledge bank' back to people (access and retrieval).

Knowledge can therefore flow from supplier to user (from person to person, or team to team) in two ways.

The most direct (the upper left arrow on Figure 1.2) is through direct communication and dialogue. Face-to-face dialogue, or dialogue via an online communication system, is an extremely effective means of knowledge transfer. This method allows vast amounts of detailed knowledge to be transferred, and the context for that knowledge to be explored. It allows direct coaching, observation and demonstration. However, it is very localised. The transfer takes place in one place at a time, involving only the people in the conversation. For all its effectiveness as a transfer method, it is not efficient. For direct communication and dialogue to be the only knowledge transfer mechanism within an

Figure 1.2 Knowledge flow from supplier to user

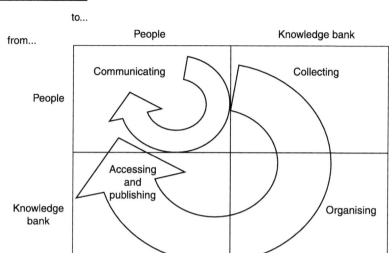

organisation would require a high level of travel and discussion, and may only be practical in a small team working from a single office where travelling is not an issue (for example a regional sales team that meets on a regular basis). This may be the only practical approach to the transfer of uncodifiable knowledge – that knowledge that cannot be written down (which Polyani would call 'tacit'). However, it should not be the only mechanism of knowledge transfer, nor should knowledge be stored only as tacit knowledge in people's heads. Using people's memories as the primary place for storing knowledge is a very risky strategy. Memories are unreliable, people forget, misremember or post-rationalise. People leave the company, retire or join the competition. For example, what is the staff turnover in your team? Your division? Your company? How much knowledge is leaving your organisation in the heads of the departing people? There needs to be a more secure storage mechanism for crucial knowledge and a more efficient means of transfer than just dialogue.

The less direct flow of knowledge (the larger, lower right arrow on Figure 1.2) is through codification and capture of the knowledge, storage in some sort of 'knowledge bank' and retrieval of the knowledge when needed. The transfer is lower bandwidth than direct communication, as it is difficult to write down more than a fragment of what you know. No dialogue is possible and demonstrations are restricted to recorded demonstrations, e.g. using video files. Transfer of knowledge by this means is not very effective. However, the knowledge need only be captured once to be accessed and reused hundreds of times, so it is an efficient method of transferring knowledge widely. The knowledge is secure against memory loss or loss of personnel. This approach is ideal for codifiable knowledge with a wide user base. For example, the widespread transfer of basic cooking knowledge is best done through publishing cookery books. It is also ideal for knowledge that is used intermittently, such as knowledge of office moves or knowledge of major acquisitions. These events may not happen again for a few years, by which time the individuals involved will have forgotten the details of what happened, if it is not captured and stored.

These two approaches to knowledge transfer are sometimes called the *connect* approach (the smaller arrow), where knowledge is transferred by connecting people, and the *collect* approach (the larger arrow), where knowledge is transferred by collecting, storing, organising and retrieving it. Each method has advantages and disadvantages, as summarised in Table 1.1. Effective knowledge management strategies need to address both of these methods of knowledge transfer. Each has its place; each complements the other.

Table 1.1	The connect and collect approaches to knowledge transfer	
Approach	**Connect**	**Collect**
Advantages	■ very effective ■ allows transfer of non-codifiable knowledge ■ allows socialisation ■ allows the knowledge user to gauge how much they trust the supplier ■ easy and cheap	■ allows systematic capture ■ creates a secure store for knowledge ■ very efficient; knowledge can be captured once and accessed many times
Disadvantages	■ risky; human memory is an unreliable knowledge store ■ inefficient; people can only be in one place at a time ■ people often don't realise what they know until it's captured	■ some knowledge cannot be effectively captured and codified ■ capturing requires skill and resource ■ captured knowledge can become impersonal

Table 1.1	The connect and collect approaches to knowledge transfer *(cont'd)*	
Types of knowledge suitable for this form of transfer	■ ephemeral, rapidly changing knowledge, which would be out of date as soon as it's written ■ knowledge of continual operations, where there is a large, constant community ■ knowledge needed by only a few	■ stable mature knowledge ■ knowledge of intermittent or rare events ■ high-value knowledge ■ knowledge with a large user base
Comments	■ One traditional approach to knowledge management is to leave knowledge in the heads of experts. This is a risky and inefficient strategy.	■ A strategy based only on capture will miss out on the socialisation that is needed for culture change, and may fail to address some of the less codifiable knowledge.

People, process, technology and governance

Systems for managing anything need to address the triple aspects of people, process and technology (see Figure 1.3). Each of these is a key enabler for any management system.

For example, a financial management system requires people (accountants, financial managers, commercial managers), processes (budgeting, accounting, financial auditing), and technology (SAP, Sage, Quicken, spreadsheets, calculators).

Similarly, a knowledge management system needs people to be assigned roles and responsibilities; processes for knowledge identification, capture, access and sharing; and technology for the storage, organisation and retrieval of knowledge.

The system of people, processes and technology will operate within a framework of corporate governance, which fosters a culture that supports the system. Financial management systems will work within a culture focused on the effective management of finances, where money is treated as company property rather than the property of the team or project, where wasting money is seen as a bad thing and where a project is not seen as being properly managed unless financial management is up to standard. This

Figure 1.3   The enablers of knowledge management

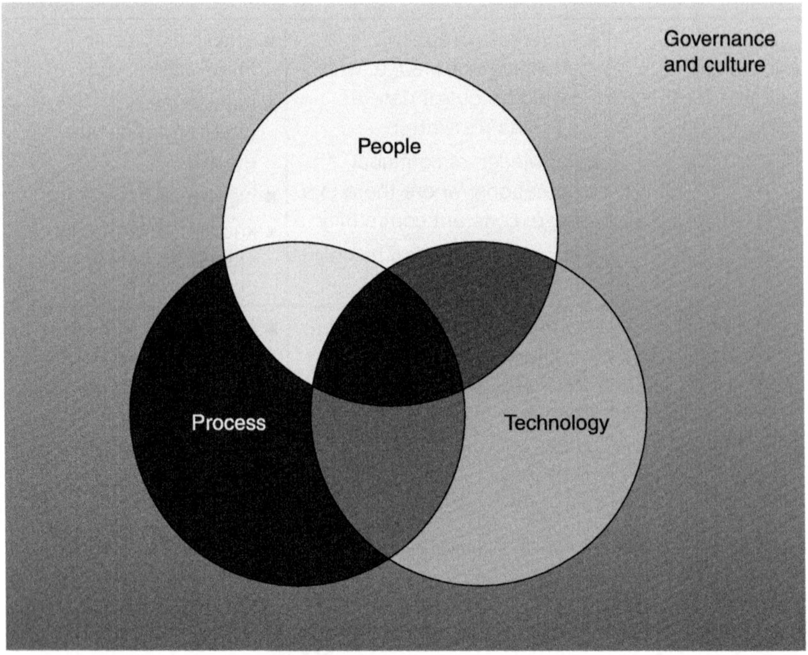

culture will be reinforced by a governance system, where the company rules for financial management are well defined and performance against these rules is audited and reported. If people don't follow the rules, their future in the company is limited. Similarly, knowledge management systems will work in a culture where knowledge is seen to be important, where knowledge is treated as company property rather than the property of the team or project, where wasting knowledge is seen as a bad thing and where a project is not seen as being properly managed unless knowledge management is up to standard. This culture will be reinforced by a governance system, where the company rules for knowledge management are well defined and performance against these rules is measured and reported. If people don't follow the rules, their future in the company is limited.

The 'learning before, during and after' model

The models presented in Figures 1.2 and 1.3 address the flow of knowledge from supplier to user and the components that need to be in

Figure 1.4 The 'learn before, during and after' model

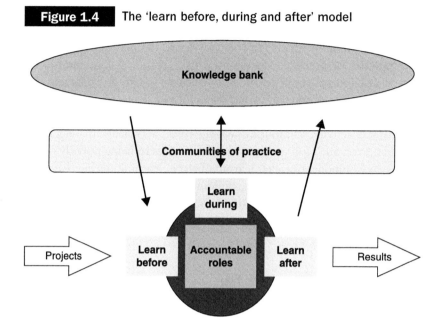

place to allow this to happen. Figure 1.4 introduces one further model, which describes how knowledge management activities can fit within the cycle of business activity.

The management of knowledge, like the management of anything else, needs to be systematic rather than ad hoc, and needs to be tied into the business cycle. In any business, where business activities have a beginning and an end, knowledge can be addressed at three points. You can learn at the start of the activity, so that the activity begins from a state of complete knowledge ('learning before'). You can learn during the activity, so that plans can be changed and adapted as new knowledge becomes available ('learning during'). Finally, you can learn at the end of the activity, so that knowledge is captured for future use ('learning after'). This model of 'learn before, during and after' was developed in BP during the 1990s, and we remember drawing the first diagram of this model in Shepperton, UK, in 1997. The 'learn before, during and after' cycle also appears to have been developed independently in several other organisations (Shell, for example, refer to it as 'Ask/Learn/Share').

However, there is more to the model than just the 'learn before, during and after' cycle. The knowledge generated from the project needs to be stored somewhere, in some sort of knowledge bank. Knowledge can be deposited in the bank at the end of the project and accessed from the bank at the start of the next project. Knowledge packaged and stored in the knowledge bank can be considered to be knowledge assets.

The final components of the framework are the people components. Communities of practice, communities of purpose or communities of interest (Chapter 4) need to be established to create and manage the knowledge assets. Knowledge roles (Chapter 6) need to be created in the business, to make sure that knowledge management is embedded in the business activity. Without knowledge roles, knowledge management becomes 'everyone's job' and very quickly reverts to being nobody's job.

This six-component model (learning before, learning during, learning after, building knowledge assets, building communities of practice and establishing business roles) is a robust model that creates value wherever it is applied.

The business need for knowledge management

This section looks at the business justification for knowledge management and where some of the value may lie. It also addresses the identification of the crucial knowledge that needs to be managed and looks at the lifecycle of knowledge within an organisation.

Business justification is crucial. If you can't clearly articulate the need for knowledge management you should not be doing it. You shouldn't be doing knowledge management only because you think it's a cool, good or fashionable thing to do. You should be able to clearly outline the business reason for doing it. This section outlines two business reasons for managing knowledge: reducing the learning curve and bringing everybody up to the benchmark, both of which will have a positive effect on the bottom line.

Knowledge and performance

There is an old saying – 'It's easy when you know how.'

Any task is easy to perform, if you have the know-how. Knowledge management consists of making sure that the teams and individuals have the know-how they need to enable them to make effective decisions and so to improve their performance. Knowledge feeds performance and knowledge is also derived from performance. If your performance on a task or project is better than it was the previous time, then you have learned something. Your know-how has increased and that know-how should be identified, analysed, codified (if possible) and disseminated to other teams. The higher your level of knowledge, the higher your level of performance. You learn from performance and you perform by applying the knowledge you have learned. (The word 'you' in this paragraph can be singular, referring to an individual, or collective, referring to a project team or community of practice.) Performance and learning can form a closed loop.

The knowledge/performance loop shown in Figure 1.5 shows the close link between these two elements and it is fairly obvious from this link that knowledge management and performance management are also strongly linked. Knowledge management is far easier to apply in an organisation with good consistent performance metrics, a performance culture, performance measurement, reporting and target-setting, and internal benchmarking. In an organisation like this, the effects of increased knowledge will be obvious and the suppliers of knowledge (the higher performers) can be identified, as well as the customers for that knowledge (the lower performers, new recruits or people new in the role).

Where performance is less easy to measure, knowledge management can still be applied, but it will be more difficult to make it systematic and embedded in the business process and it will be considerably more difficult to measure the benefits.

Figure 1.5 **The link between knowledge and performance**

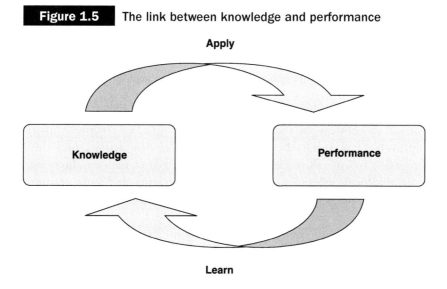

Your knowledge management system and your performance management system should be aligned; they should operate on the same scale (cover the same areas of the company) and to the same frequency. Generally, the periodicity of target-setting and performance-measuring should match the periodicity of learning and review. If weekly sales targets are set, then learning should be reviewed on a weekly basis. If targets are set on a monthly basis, then they should be reviewed, and learning collected, on a monthly basis.

The learning curve

The concept of the learning curve is well established. The longer you do something and the more times you repeat something, the better you get at it. A team that works together on a regular basis will find that over time they get better, their sales figures go up, their bid success ratio rises and their market share increases.

Figure 1.6a represents a team that runs a programme of six activities. Over time they get better at these types of activity and the results improve. By the time they get to the fifth and sixth sales, marketing or bid project, they are working at their maximum capacity. The one thing that they have at the end of this curve, which they did not have at the beginning, is knowledge. They have gained know-how, experience, guidelines and heuristics for running this sort of activity.

If they manage their knowledge by concentrating on 'learning during' the programme and transferring the knowledge from one project to the next, they may be able to learn faster. This is shown diagrammatically by in the solid bars in Figure 1.6b. Here the overall value of the results from six activities has been increased by steepening the learning curve.

If they also 'learn before' the programme, by bringing in knowledge and experience from similar previous programmes, they don't have to start at the bottom of the learning curve. Figure 1.6c shows further improvement in results by learning before the first activity and then continuing to learn through the sequence. What often happens, however, is that this focus on learning will also drive innovation, and improvements in maximum efficiency may result. The teams may exceed the maximum performance they otherwise would have achieved, as shown in Figure 1.6d, where overall improvements of about 20 per cent have been achieved.

Figure 1.6 The learning curve

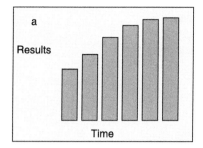

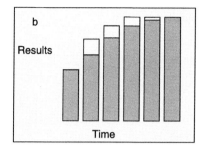

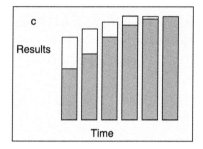

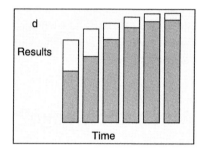

Benchmarking

Another way to look at the value of knowledge management is to observe the transfer of best practices from one part of the business to another, as shown in Figure 1.7.

If you can measure and compare the performance of different teams in business units, you can identify the better performers and the poorer ones. For example, Figure 1.7a shows the performance results for six different teams. High bars equate to good performance, such as high sales, high market share or high win ratio.

Teams A and D are the best performers, with A setting the benchmark, and E and F are the worst. If all of these teams exchange knowledge and the poorer performers learn from the better performers, the overall performance should improve, as shown in Figure 1.7b. All of the teams have improved and C has set a new benchmark. Considerable value has been added to the organisation.

Internal benchmarking metrics can therefore be a powerful means of measuring the value of knowledge management and of identifying the knowledge suppliers and the knowledge users (in Figure 1.7a, teams A

Figure 1.7   Knowledge management and benchmarking

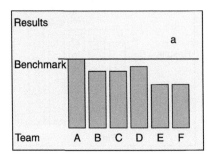
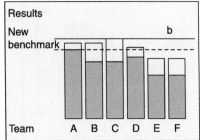

and D are primarily knowledge suppliers, and teams B, C, E and F are knowledge users, although to an extent all teams both supply and use knowledge).

Which knowledge?

The models shown in the previous two sections describe where the business value of knowledge lies, but not all knowledge is of equal value. Some knowledge will be crucial to your business and some will be largely irrelevant. Some knowledge drives your core competencies, while some can be conveniently outsourced. One key component of setting your knowledge management strategy within a business, or your knowledge management plan for a project, is to define *which knowledge* – which knowledge is needed, which knowledge needs to be acquired, which knowledge will be generated, which knowledge needs to be captured and codified, etc.

Figure 1.8 shows a framework for deciding which knowledge to address and how to manage it. You can start to divide knowledge topics into four areas if you look at two components: the level of in-house knowledge that currently exists and the level of in-house need for that knowledge.

- Where an important area of knowledge is new or rapidly evolving and the level of in-house knowledge is not yet very high, you are at the top of the learning curve and your focus should be on rapid learning.

- Where an important area of knowledge is new or rapidly evolving and the level of in-house knowledge is high, you are looking at areas of competitive competence. You know a lot, in a new area, and your focus should be on development and implementation of best

Figure 1.8 Categorisation of knowledge

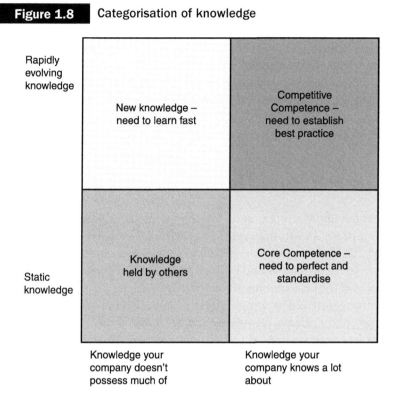

Rapidly evolving knowledge

New knowledge – need to learn fast

Competitive Competence – need to establish best practice

Knowledge held by others

Core Competence – need to perfect and standardise

Static knowledge

Knowledge your company doesn't possess much of

Knowledge your company knows a lot about

practices – on finding the best and most effective solutions and making sure people share these.

- Where an important area of knowledge is fairly mature or static and the level of in-house knowledge is high, you are looking at areas of established knowledge and core competence and your focus should be on standardising your approach.

- Where an important area of knowledge is fairly mature or static and the level of in-house knowledge is low, this is generally an area you have outsourced, perhaps to an ad agency or a market research company. Here your focus should be sharing context with these companies, so they can bring the right knowledge to bear, and also on ensuring that they have KM in place to manage the knowledge on your behalf.

An early step in development of the business knowledge management strategy or a project knowledge management plan is to identify the key knowledge areas and plot them on a matrix such as Figure 1.8. Critical knowledge for sales and marketing will be addressed in Chapter 2.

Approaches to knowledge management

The more widely you read around the topic of knowledge management, the more knowledge managers you meet and the more conferences you attend, the more you will come to realise that there are many approaches to managing knowledge. This section introduces some of these approaches, and makes the case for a holistic and systematic approach as described above.

The default approach

The default approach that many companies use is to keep knowledge in people's heads and to manage the knowledge by managing the people. Knowledge is owned by the experts and the experienced staff. Knowledge is imported to businesses and projects by assigning experienced people as members of the project team. Knowledge is transferred from site to site by transferring staff and by using company experts who fly around the world from project to project, identifying and spreading good practices.

This is a very traditional model, but it has many major failings and cannot be considered to be knowledge management. Imagine you managing your finances in this way! Imagine if the only way to fund a project was to transfer a rich person into the business or to fly individual millionaires around the world to inject funds into the business or projects they liked!

The major drawbacks of this default 'knowledge in the heads' approach are as follows:

- Experienced people can only be on one project at a time.
- Knowledge cannot be transferred until people are available for transfer.
- Experts who fly in and fly out often do not gain a good appreciation of how things are done and where the good practices lie. In particular, teams in the business may hide their failings from the company experts in order to be seen in a good light.
- The burn-out potential for the experts is very high.
- Knowledge can become almost 'fossilised' in the heads of the experts, who can end up applying the solutions of yesterday to the problems of today.
- When the expert leaves, retires, has a heart attack or is recruited by the competition, the knowledge goes with them.

Unfortunately, for the experts and the experienced people, this can be an attractive model and was stereotypical behaviour for specialist bidders and marketers for many years. It can be very exciting travelling the world, with everyone wanting your assistance. It is like early Hollywood movie scenes with the US Cavalry riding over the horizon to save the wagon train at the last minute. Knowledge management, however, would make sure that the wagon train did not get into trouble in the first place. As one expert said recently, 'If you could fly off to Russia and be a hero, or sit behind your desk and capture knowledge, what would you rather do?'

Partial approaches

There are many partial approaches to knowledge management, whereby some components of the model are applied and others omitted. These sometimes have partial success, but nothing like the success that might be delivered by a more consistent, systematic and holistic solution. Some of the common partial solutions are listed below:

- A technology-led approach – Here an organisation commonly builds or buys a 'knowledge base' or a 'collaboration platform' where explicit knowledge can be stored, searched and shared with other teams. Such technology can be a key component of a holistic solution and addresses the technology components of the capture, organise and retrieve boxes of Figure 1.3. However, unless you address the people and process technologies as well, the database will either remain empty, be sporadically filled only from selected activities or projects, or will fail to address the aspects of systematic reuse. Many organisations fall into the trap of applying a technology-led approach (possibly because it is relatively easy to buy and install a piece of technology), but find that the technology is unused. Technology is rarely the single barrier to knowledge management, and implementing technology alone is rarely sufficient. If technology were the barrier, you would see people in the organisation struggling to exchange knowledge with substandard technology such as telephones, Word documents and paper files. It is much more common to find the barrier is lack of culture, lack of process or lack of accountabilities.

- An E2.0-led approach – This is a variant of the technology-led approach, whereby an organisation introduces a collaboration toolkit of workspaces, blogs, wikis and discussion forums. Again, these technologies are very powerful in supporting knowledge management, but they alone will not deliver knowledge management. Unfortunately, many companies roll them out and then expect KM to emerge spontaneously. It doesn't, because the people, process and governance aspects have again been ignored.

- A community-led approach – A common partial approach is to implement communities of practice or communities of purpose (see Chapter 4) as the primary knowledge management solution. Knowledge is transferred primarily in the tacit realm, along the short connect arrow in Figure 1.2. Sometimes the communities also take ownership of explicit knowledge, so the longer collect arrow is also addressed, and if this happens, you certainly are developing a more complete knowledge management solution. However, unless the business teams and business projects are also involved in knowledge management, the 'learn before, during and after' cycle in Figure 1.4 never gets deployed and knowledge management therefore becomes decoupled from the cycles of business activity. Many companies introduce communities of practice as the 'silver bullet' – the only thing they need to manage knowledge – while in fact communities are only one dimension of a multidimensional solution. They are, however, a good place to start, and Mars (Chapter 9), Aon and others have had great success with KM strategies that start with communities and then broaden.

- A content-led approach – Here an organisation introduces document management or content management as its approach to knowledge management. It assumes that the greater part of knowledge is held in explicit form in documents and that if these documents can be organised, stored, searched and retrieved (perhaps using techniques such as data mining, text summarisation and natural-language searching), knowledge will be shared. Unfortunately, this is an extremely ineffective way of managing knowledge. Many documents contain far more data and information than knowledge, and unless there is a systematic owned process for knowledge identification and capture, most of the knowledge will never make it into document form in the first place. In addition, unless there is a systematic owned process for knowledge validation, distillation and organisation, knowledge will become diluted and irretrievable in a sea of irrelevant documentation. Finally, this approach deals with explicit knowledge and will not address those components of knowledge that have to remain tacit because they are uncodifiable.

The holistic approach

The approach to knowledge management advocated in this book is a holistic approach, which addresses all of the dimensions. The models shown in Figures 1.2–1.4 are combined into a system that addresses:

- tacit knowledge (in people's heads) and explicit knowledge (in the knowledge bank);
- knowledge communication, capture, storage and retrieval;
- people, process, technology and cultural aspects;
- learning before, during and after;
- project teams and communities of practice.

The rest of this book will look at how this system can be applied to sales and marketing.

Cultural issues

We previously discussed how knowledge management requires a profound shift in individual and corporate attitudes to knowledge. In Western society, knowledge is seen as an individual attribute. At school, children are tested on what they know and any attempt to access the knowledge of others is seen as cheating. In professional life, people often feel a sense of pride in their own skills, knowledge and achievements, and sometimes would rather solve a problem themselves, just for the challenge, than seek an existing solution. The individual's knowledge and experience can also be felt to be a personal asset and a hedge against being made redundant, replaced or outsourced.

When people feel this way, there can be many cultural barriers to knowledge management. These include the following:

- *knowledge is power:* 'if I tell you what I know, I lose some of my personal power';
- *not invented here:* 'your knowledge is not as trustworthy as mine';
- *drive to create:* 'it's more fun finding the answer for myself, than using someone else's answer';
- *fear of exposure:* 'I am not going to share my failures with you, it might make me look bad';
- *fear of exposure (2):* 'I am not going to ask for help and advice, it makes me look as if I don't know what I am doing';

- *not my job:* 'I am paid for delivering results, not for sharing results with others';
- *not my job (2):* 'KM is not in my KPIs (key performance indicators, or key objectives), and not in my incentives. Why should I bother?'

Any organisation that sees the business value in knowledge management (i.e. reducing the learning curve, bringing everyone up to the best performance standard, as discussed earlier), needs to address these cultural issues. A new culture needs to be fostered, as follows:

- *shared knowledge is greater power:* 'if we share what we know, we will meet our individual and strategic targets';
- *invented here is not good enough:* 'we know we don't know everything, and will look around for additional knowledge before every task';
- *drive to perform:* 'it may be more fun to create the solution, but if a better solution exists, we will use it' (saving time by applying existing solutions creates time for real innovation);
- *fear of underperforming:* 'I am going to ask for help and advice because I want to make my job as easy and safe as possible';
- *fear of underperforming (2):* 'if something went wrong on my project, I am going to make sure it never happens to any future projects';
- *it's my job:* 'I am paid for delivering results, and that includes KM results';
- *it's my job (2):* 'KM is a prime enabler to delivering my KPIs, and thus my incentives. It's part of the job'.

The more a team is driven by performance (their own team performance as well as the organisational performance) and empowered to seek solutions, the more readily they will embrace knowledge management as an aid to performance. Managers can reinforce this by encouraging and rewarding knowledge-seeking and knowledge-sharing, by setting the expectation that every team will seek to improve on the best of past performance, by empowering teams to seek the best solutions from across the organisation (and outside) and by minimising the effects of any internal competition between teams, projects and business units.

These thoughts are expanded further in Chapter 7, which covers culture and governance.

Notes

1. Milton, Nick (2004) *Knowledge Management for Teams and Projects*. Oxford: Chandos Publishing.
2. Young, Tom (2009) *Knowledge Management for Services, Operations and Manufacturing*. Oxford: Chandos Publishing.
3. Senge, Peter M. (2004) Conference Proceedings of KM Asia, Singapore, 2–4 November.
4. Polanyi, Michael (1966) *The Tacit Dimension*. First published Doubleday & Co. Reprinted Peter Smith, Gloucester, MA, 1983. Chapter 1: 'Tacit Knowing'.
5. Nonaka, Ikujiro and Takeuchi, Hirotaka (1995) *The Knowledge Creating Company: How Japanese companies create the dynamics of innovation*. New York: Oxford University Press, p. 284.

Notes

1.

2.

3.

4.

5.

The sales and marketing context

In this chapter, we will look at the context for knowledge management within sales and marketing and at the types of knowledge that should be addressed.

We need to state up front that there is more than one sales and marketing context. The work of the lone salesperson in a one-to-one relationship with a buyer is very different from that of a marketing team working together on a global campaign based on the latest market research. As we look at the different contexts, we will focus on three main areas:

- the distributed salesforce, working with buyers and customers, delivering to sales targets;
- the bid team, developing and delivering large-scale bids, often in response to an invitation to tender;
- the marketing team, responsible for planning, delivering and evaluating marketing campaigns.

For each of these, we will look at the way they work and at the knowledge they need. There are other contexts as well of course – the store-based salespeople, door-to-door selling, the traders who buy and sell commodities, telesales and many others – but these three probably cover between them most of the KM issues for sales and marketing.

The sales force

The sales force usually work as individuals, but often these individuals can be grouped into teams covering specific regions and specific products or product ranges for their organisation. They may be selling FMCGs (fast-moving consumer goods) such as clothing or pharmaceuticals to buyers in high street chains (such as Mars in Chapter 9), they may be selling IT solutions to blue-chip businesses (like BT in Chapter 7) or they may be selling cars to fleet buyers in major multinationals. They work to sales targets and are often highly motivated and incentivised to meet those targets. They spend a lot of their time with the buyers and customers and relatively little time at 'head office' with the rest of the team.

The sales force needs the following knowledge:

- *Knowledge of how to sell* – They need the basic knowledge of the sales process, such as relationship-building, negotiation and closing. This can be taught in theory, but the knowledge is really only acquired through practice, for example through role-play and coaching, as well as on-the-job learning. As one sales director told us, 'we always do a lot of scenario planning. Before reviews I sit with my team and I plan what is the worst that might happen and how do we combat it? What is the most likely case and how do we combat this? What is the best case and how do we maximise the outcome?'

- *Knowledge of pricing* – Sometimes the price of an item is flexible, with the potential for offers and promotions such as 'buy one, get one free'. The sales force need to know the pricing strategy, the pricing options and how to sell the benefits of the pricing approach to the buyer. This knowledge needs to be provided to the sales force by the experts in the sales organisation, who themselves rely on input from the sales force. Pricing strategies can usefully be shared between sales forces in different regions and different countries.

- *Knowledge of product* – The sales force need to know the details of the product and to be rapidly briefed about any new products that are developed. In the conversation with the buyer, the sales person has to be the product expert. This knowledge comes from the product development unit and may also be informed by feedback from customers and consumers. One firm producing motor oil products actually delivers regular training ('Motoroil 101') to its sales and marketing departments to bring them up to speed in new products.

- *Knowledge of the consumers and their behaviour* – This includes knowledge of consumer wants and buying habits and how to influence them, through display, through promotions and through education. The sales person selling to a retailer, for example, must be the recognised category expert and understand the category shopper better than the buyer and better than the competing companies. 'One thing that we offer is our understanding of the local consumer and we need to use that knowledge to advise the retailer,' said one sales manager. This knowledge can be used to sell the products and brands better, to build more 'shoppable' displays and help grow sales for the retailer and thus for the sales force. The sales rep starts to act as an expert consultant, offering a knowledge-based service.

- *Knowledge of their sales to that buyer and the overall market (or competition?)* – They need to know the sales data, the margins and the trend. This knowledge will be delivered by the central sales organisation, based on studies and on aggregated sales data from across the firm. One sales manager told us, 'We have to know our data and information much better than the buyers do. They will use a set of information on how much they buy and sell from us; we need to know these data far better than they do.' If the buyer understands the data better than the seller, the seller is at a disadvantage. This knowledge needs to cover the buyer's competitors' data as well, if possible. The sales rep selling to a retailer will probably have data for all of the retailer's competitors and although they cannot give away any specifics, they can talk about trends and share insights in terms of what is going on across the overall marketplace. This knowledge is much appreciated by the buyer and becomes an added service the sales force can offer.

- *Knowledge of the buyers and the buying companies* – The best sales work through mutual advantage, so that both the buyer and the seller benefit from the deal. Therefore the sales force need knowledge of the buying organisation and its goals and objectives, as well as those of the individual buyers. The sales organisation needs to seek to understand their big customers, their game plan and drivers, and develop and define a customer profile and a unique customer strategy based on that profile, which is shared with and understood by the entire sales force. Although much of this knowledge comes from the sales force themselves, it will again be aggregated by the central organisation.

- *Knowledge of the production capacity of the organisation* – There is no point in selling something that can't be delivered, so the sales force need to know what can be produced for and delivered to the client. Again, this knowledge needs to be delivered to the sales force by knowledge transfer along the internal supply chain, and needs to be incorporated into sales targets.

A knowledge management framework for a sales organisation will probably contain the following elements:

Processes

The processes and technologies marked below in bold are described in detail in Chapters 3 and 5:

- **coaching** and **training** (including role-play and scenario planning);
- regular **knowledge exchanges** and mini-**peer assists** during meetings of the regional team and the wider sales **community**;
- creation of **knowledge assets** on pricing, consumer insights and dealing with buyers (especially major accounts). These knowledge assets will have been developed through **interviews** with key successful sales staff.

Technology

- access to the sales **community** while on the road, to share updates and ask questions;
- access to customer-related and account-related data while on the road and in the office;
- provision of knowledge of products; this has to be supported by a mobile-enabled **knowledge base**.

The bid team

A bid team is also involved in selling, but selling in a very different context to that of the field sales force. The task of compiling a modern bid document should not be underestimated. The cost of tendering can run into very substantial figures. The bid team works as a team. Some organisations have a full-time team to work on all bids, while others create new teams to service each bid. We have worked with bid teams in the nuclear industry selling services for decommissioning nuclear power stations, bid teams in the service industry bidding for major private finance initiative (PFI) contracts, such as new schools and hospitals, and oil and gas teams bidding for the right to explore acreage. In each case, the team is looking to sell its service to the client, in competition with rival companies. Bidding is not a continuous operation; it is episodic and each bid can be considered to be a project. The metric for the bid is simple – win or lose (although the magnitude of the win is also important, as the service needs to make a profit. As one bid manager told us, 'If we get it wrong on a major bid, we can get it wrong for the next 25 years.') However, the best bid team has a high conversion ratio – the ratio of won bids to lost bids – and will convert more bids to contracts than other teams.

A bid team needs the following knowledge:

- *Knowledge of the bidding and procurement process* – They have to know how to tender, how prequalification works, how bids are awarded and so on. This is fairly basic knowledge, but needs tailoring for each specific market and each specific bid process. Does the client have a preferred contract style, for example? Do they require certain prequalification conditions? What aspects of the bid document are most important and will be awarded most points in the bid evaluation process? The bid team needs to acquire this knowledge from previous teams operating in this market or with this client.

- *Knowledge of the client* – They need to understand the needs of the client and their business drivers. The successful bid will be one that speaks directly to the client's needs and that uses examples and references that the client will understand and appreciate. This knowledge will come from those who interact with the client – maybe the sales force, maybe staff with a history of working with that client or people already delivering a service to the client.

- *Knowledge of which bids may be coming up in the future* – There is huge advantage in being networked into the market, so that you have advance notice of forthcoming projects before the request for tender is issued. You can gain some advance notice and do some research before the bid even begins. Again, this knowledge comes from your colleagues already working in the market.

- *Knowledge of how to construct a bid document* – Creating a bid document is a complex project requiring collaboration between many people and the cost can be considerable. There is huge value to the organisation in being able to construct bids quickly, effectively and efficiently, perhaps reusing powerful content from previous bids. Again, the bid team needs to acquire this knowledge and content from previous teams operating in this market.

- *Knowledge of the product or service* – This is crucial and this knowledge provides the core of the document. Very often, the knowledge and experience of the bidder is a strong selling point and this experience needs to be clear in the document. You also need to make it clear that you have a good knowledge management system in place and that you can therefore guarantee that the service or product you are offering will include the best knowledge of your company. This knowledge comes from those already delivering that product or service.

- *Knowledge of pricing* – This is crucial for a big bid. If the pricing is too low, the company may make a loss for a long time. If the pricing is too high, they may not win the bid at all. This knowledge comes from past history of bidding and from teams already delivering the service (and who can therefore warn of hidden costs and hidden risks), as well as any market intelligence that might be available.

A knowledge management framework for bid teams will therefore contain the following elements:

Processes

The processes and technologies marked below in bold are described in detail in Chapters 3 and 5:

- knowledge capture (**retrospects**) at the end of each bid;
- **after action reviews** during bid preparation;
- **peer assist** at the start of each new bid, involving previous bid teams, people currently involved in delivering the service that is being bid and anyone with detailed knowledge of the client;
- creation of **knowledge assets** on bidding;
- creation of a bidding **community of practice**, which may meet on a regular basis for **knowledge exchange.**

Technology

- a **knowledge base,** including a historical knowledge base of previous bids and relevant pieces of 'boilerplate' text that can be reused in future bids;
- a **forum** for the bidding community of practice;
- a **yellow pages,** to allow the bid team to identify the correct people to attend the peer assist.

The marketing team

Marketing is about successful brand-building for a product or service and so generating the conditions for sale. Marketing can be done on a variety of scales. At one end of the scale, an account manager working with a client should always be on the lookout for opportunities to market new products and new services to that particular client. At the other end of the scale lies mass marketing, where the marketers seek to build brands that address specific consumer wants. For knowledge management purposes, we will focus on mass marketing in this section and refer you to the Ordnance Survey case study in Chapter 10 for a discussion of the role of the account manager in the marketing/sales pipeline.

Mass product marketing is a team task, delivered through marketing projects and campaigns. As in a bid, a marketing project has a beginning, a middle and an end, and often in a global organisation multiple marketing projects are going on all over the world, marketing the same or similar brands across multiple markets. Marketing is fertile ground for the creation of communities of practice, and marketing communities are seen in many organisations, such as Siemens, Coca-Cola, BP, Unilever and Mars (Chapter 9).

A marketing team needs the following knowledge:

- *Knowledge of the marketing process* – They have to know how marketing works and how the marketing process and the marketing cycle are applied within their particular organisation. This is often codified centrally within the organisation; for example, SABMiller have codified their marketing approach in their 'Marketing Way', which they describe as 'a toolkit for helping businesses to "own the growth" by sharpening their skills in analysing and segmenting their markets, identifying the profitable opportunities and deciding where and how to concentrate their efforts'.[1]

- *Knowledge of the market* – They need to understand the characteristics of the particular market, including the number of consumers – current and potential; the types of consumer (consumer segmentation); the trends in market size in terms of value and volume; the market share of each major competitor and brand (including their own); the market segments (premium, mid-price, economy); the routes to market, and the regulatory framework (where applicable).

- *Knowledge of how to market to a particular segment* – They need to know what strategy and approach to take to improve the standing of their brand in the market. For example, do they invest in trade marketing, TV advertisements, print advertisements, promotions such as 'buy one, get one free' or online marketing? This knowledge can easily be shared between different markets around the world through the marketing community of practice.

- *Knowledge of agencies* – Much of the market research and the creation of marketing materials are done through agencies. The marketing teams need to know how to choose an agency and how best to manage the interaction between the marketing team and the agency. This knowledge comes through experience.

- *Knowledge of the product or service* – Marketing needs a good understanding of the product and its unique selling points. With technical products, this understanding has to come from the product development department and generally they will document details of the product, to be stored in the product database.

- *Knowledge of how the consumer perceives the product or service* – Marketing needs to understand whether or not consumers like their product and why. Marketing needs feedback from the consumers, either through market research, from sales, from technical support, from their consumer hotline or from consumer forums and consumer communities.

- *Knowledge of specific activities, such as product launch* – Product launch is a major milestone in the life of a new product, which can have a significant positive or negative impact on product sales, depending on how well it has been planned and executed. It's therefore essential to develop knowledge in the team of how to do this. This knowledge will come from lessons from previous product launches and analysis of lessons from previous product launches. The starting point of these lessons will be the careful tracking and analysis of sales after product launch.

A knowledge management framework for marketing teams will therefore contain the following elements:

Processes

- **peer assist** at the start of new marketing campaigns in new markets or for a very new and different product;
- knowledge capture (**retrospects**) at the end of each marketing campaign (perhaps once the uplift in sales has been measured);

- **after-action reviews** after major milestones, such as product launch;
- creation of **knowledge assets** on the marketing process (such as the SABMiller Marketing Way mentioned above);
- creation of a marketing **community of practice** or **communities of purpose** (or a number of communities, each focusing on a product category or a specific brand), for the exchange of knowledge and good practice in marketing and for exchanging marketing materials that others can adapt and reuse;
- creation of **product-based communities**, where knowledge of specific products can be exchanged along the supply chain.

Technology

- a **knowledge library** of marketing materials (see Chapter 5);
- a **market database**, containing data on market size and shares, sales figures and data from consumer research;
- a **product database** containing information and/or data on specific products;
- a **forum** for the marketing community of practice;
- forums or a mechanism for discussion among the product communities;
- a **yellow pages**, to allow the marketing team to identify the experts and members of other marketing teams from around the world.

The interface between product development, manufacturing, marketing and sales

Chapter 10 discusses a case history of knowledge exchange at the Ordnance Survey along the marketing/sales supply chain, which is in itself a subset of a longer process of product development, marketing and sales. Knowledge needs to flow in many directions along the whole supply chain:

- Product development needs to understand the market and so needs knowledge from marketing and sales in order to develop products that fill a market need.

- Marketing and sales both need knowledge from product development of new products and forthcoming products.
- Marketing, sales and product development all need knowledge about the customer regarding what the customers do, will and would buy.
- Other departments, such as technical support and manufacturing, also need to be in the knowledge loop (see Figure 2.1).
- Finally and most importantly, the entire supply chain needs to develop knowledge about 'how to develop, launch, market and sell new products'.

As Graeme Smith says in Chapter 10, 'As an intense human activity, customer supply chains are wholly dependent on knowledge and require social network activity to transfer that knowledge to the point of need.' The knowledge that he is referring to is knowledge of the supply chain activity, namely 'how to create, market and sell products and services for maximum company return'.

This knowledge is a fundamental requirement for any manufacturing and selling organisation. This knowledge is difficult to manage because it needs to cross organisational discipline silos, unlike any of the other examples given above, which operate within individual disciplines.

A knowledge management framework for the entire supply chain will therefore contain the following elements:

Figure 2.1   Flow of knowledge along the internal supply chain

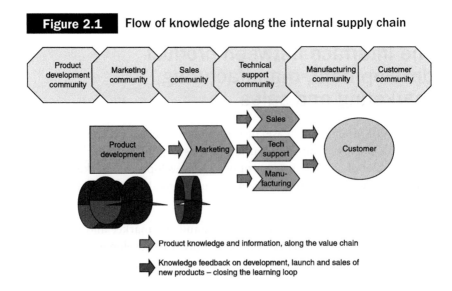

Product knowledge and information, along the value chain

Knowledge feedback on development, launch and sales of new products – closing the learning loop

Processes

- **peer assists** at the start of new development projects, by a multidivisional new product development team, which would include R&D, supply, marketing, finance and sales;
- **knowledge capture** (**retrospects**) some time (for example one or two years) after product launch, when the real products sales can be compared with the predicted product sales, in order to draw out lessons for the entire supply chain. In some organisations this is part of the product launch review;
- creation of a **knowledge asset** on product development;
- creation of **product-based communities,** where knowledge of specific products can be exchanged along the supply chain. In some organisations the product-based community would be part of marketing.

Technology

- a **product database** containing information and/or data on specific products;
- forums or some other mechanism for discussion among the product communities.

Summary

Although sales, marketing and indeed the entire supply chain need different knowledge, the knowledge management framework that can fulfil their needs, i.e. the processes and technologies within that framework, are essentially the same.

In the next three chapters we will describe these processes and technologies in more detail and also discuss the communities and knowledge roles that need to be in place.

Note

1. *http://www.sabmiller.com/files/reports/ar2008/6_strategic/priority4.html*

3

Knowledge management processes in sales, bidding and marketing

Up to now we have talked about the different types of knowledge that would be needed by sales teams and sales reps, by marketing teams, by bid teams and by the entire supply chain, and we have also suggested some of the knowledge management processes and technologies that could be used as part of a knowledge management framework for these teams and individuals. In this chapter we will discuss the processes in enough detail in order for you to be able to apply them within your own sales, bidding or marketing context.

We will start with the large-scale processes and work towards the smaller scale.

Figure 3.1   Knowledge management processes

Peer assist

Peer assist is a tried and proven method for learning before a piece of activity, such as bid preparation, a product launch or a major new marketing campaign. It is a meeting before embarking on activity, where a bid team or a marketing team ask for help and advice from others around the organisation with relevant experience, to ensure that they start from a full state of knowledge. It is a 'knowledge-seeking' exercise; an example is 'knowledge pull', where the team that needs the knowledge 'pulls' it to themselves. The peer assist is conducted in the early stages before things become 'locked in'.

The peer assist is attended by the marketing team or the bid team (the 'host team') and a set of peers from around the organisation, from other teams or from the corporate centre, who have experience and knowledge to share ('visiting peers'). The host team will have selected a team of visiting peers by using a corporate yellow pages to find people with relevant skills and experience, by asking the company experts for nominations or by personal networking. A peer assist is not the same as an expert review, the intention being to invite peers to assist you rather than corporate experts to review you.

The ideal structure for a peer assist is a four-part structure:

- In the first part of the meeting, after the introductions and welcome, the host team explains what they know about the activity they have planned, the nature of the bid or the nature of the market, the strategic objectives and any local constraints they may be working under.

- In the second part of the meeting, the visiting peers discuss their knowledge and experience from previous activities of this sort and may even present details of successful bids or marketing campaigns.

- In the third part of the meeting, the host team and the visiting peers go through a process of dialogue, often in small groups, as they attempt to use past experience to address the host team's issues.

- In the final part of the meeting, the visiting peers confer, then feed back their recommendations to the host team.

The success of peer assists depends on the following factors:

- The peer assist needs clear objectives. The visiting peers are bringing their knowledge to the host team for a purpose. The clearer you can be about that purpose, the more likely it is that the peer assist will deliver value. Sample objectives might be 'develop a list of risks and issues' or 'provide a list of options for reducing the bid price by 20 per cent'.

- The peer assist should be focused on assisting. In other words, it is a meeting where the host team needs help and assistance, which is provided by the visiting peers. The host team therefore need to be open to learning and the visiting peers need to be willing to share their knowledge and experience. If the meeting falls into 'attack and defend' behaviours, it has failed its purpose. This will be most likely be achieved if 1) the peer assist is held early in the activity, before the team have selected their preferred option, and 2) the peer assist is facilitated by someone external to the project.

- The peer assist should truly involve peers, i.e. the peers of the host team. These are not meetings where you bring in experts or senior managers to review what is being proposed by the host team. People are far more open to learning from and sharing with their peers and this removes all the politics associated with management hierarchies.

You may need to incentivise both the provider and adopter of the knowledge to take time out to undertake the peer assist. The incentive for the host team is that they gain access to useful knowledge and experience. Generally the incentive for the visiting peers is that they are flattered to be asked! It is a recognition of their experience and it involves them, for a relatively short period of time, in a different challenge. In some organisations, peer assists are mandatory at the beginning of the bid process.

In Milton 2010,[1] Linda Davies of Mars Inc. explains the use of peer assist as part of their global practice group (GPG) meetings:

> One day of each meeting is spent working with the sales force in the market in which the meeting is being held. The day begins with a briefing on the local market and its structure, including the top three challenges which the business unit is currently facing. The GPG members spend a day working in smaller groups with an experienced local sales associate, looking at a broad range of retail outlets. At the end of the day the GPG reconvenes to give detailed feedback on what they see as working well in the market – how to build on the successes they see. They also give their top 10 ideas on how to address the challenges, based on lessons and experience from their own markets. In this way the host market receives positive confirmation of their success and how to build on it, plus around 30 ideas and improvement suggestions targeted at their key

challenges, based on lessons from proven, practical experience elsewhere in the world.

Another organisation held a peer assist to support its management in one country that was struggling to develop market share. The peer assist was called by the senior manager and therefore was attended by senior managers from other markets (being his peers). Early in the meeting, one of the visiting peers asked to see a copy of the local five-year business plan and there was an embarrassed silence until the local manager admitted that he didn't actually have one. Rather than criticise him for this omission, the visiting peers got together and helped him to build an excellent five-year plan that would get market share on track. One of the visiting peers, who had been taking copious notes in his notebook, commented as he left the meeting that he now had enough material to update the five-year business plan for his own market.

Knowledge exchange

The knowledge exchange process is frequently used where the organisation wants to compile best practice in a particular area by bringing together people from all over the organisation who work on that topic. A knowledge exchange is a meeting where people from several locations come together to pool what they know (in Mars, they are known as 'Show and Tell' meetings, see Chapter 9). Everybody is a provider of knowledge and everybody learns something as well. These can be very high-powered, creative meetings, often pivotal in the development of an organisation's knowledge.

Some success factors for a large knowledge exchange process are as follows:

- *Decide on the topic.* A knowledge exchange addresses a 'hot topic'. This may be a topic where teams in one area are known to have expertise that the others need; it may be a topic where all have expertise and where there is interest in seeing other good ideas; or it may be a topic where it is accepted that a more common approach would be beneficial.

- *Assign an organisation team.* A knowledge exchange can be quite a large event and needs at least two people, possibly more, to form an organisation team. People are needed to fill the following roles (although some members of the team could hold more than one of these roles):

  - find a business sponsor for the event, to provide funding and business context – someone sufficiently high-level to give legitimacy to the event;
  - an organiser to act as project manager for the knowledge exchange;
  - appoint one or more facilitators;
  - someone to handle logistics (travel, accommodation, etc.);
  - someone to coordinate recording of the event;
  - someone to package the knowledge afterwards.

- *Choose an off-site location.* At an office location, people will be distracted and may be called away to deal with urgent problems.

- *Decide on scope and objectives.* You have to be clear on the topic to be covered at the knowledge exchange. If the scope is not well defined, the event can expand out of control.

The knowledge exchange format is an exercise in organising dialogue between a large group of people. The best way to do this is to break up into smaller groups for discussion and to reconvene regularly for feedback and wider discussion. This pattern can be interspersed with group discussions for variety (especially later in the exchange, when people are comfortable with the process). The structure of the exchange itself might therefore contain the following elements:

- *Introduction to the meeting* – State the purpose of the knowledge exchange, the objectives and the ground rules, why it is important to the business, how it will be conducted, what the purpose of the recording is and what end product will be produced. Go through the agenda, discuss roles, make sure everyone understands what they are there to do.

- *Message from the business sponsor* – It can be useful to start the knowledge exchange with an introduction from the business sponsor, describing the importance of the exchange and the business need. If they cannot attend in person, ask them to record a short video message, which can be shown at the start.

- *Identification of key issues associated with the topic* – You need some way to divide up the entire topic under discussion into meaningful chunks. There are a number of ways to do this, such as dividing the process into its component parts as a flow chart or timeline, or brainstorming, grouping, sorting and ranking the key issues.

- *Dialogue around some of the issues or some of the steps, often in small breakout groups, to identify good practices* – Dialogue in one big group is possible and some of the issues can be covered this way, but you may get a more open dialogue in a smaller group. The smaller groups can discuss the same issue in parallel or you can divide the meeting into separate groups to discuss separate issues. Each issue will need a couple of hours' dialogue and 15 to 20 minutes of feedback and discussion time. Give the groups clear tasks, such as 'discuss the main learnings around this issue and what messages you would give to others based on your experience. Be prepared for one of your group to give a 10-minute flipchart-based summary of your learnings, back in the main room in two hours' time.' For each group, somebody needs to be appointed as facilitator and somebody needs to be appointed as recorder or 'scribe'. The facilitator needs to get this dialogue going and steer it to delivering valuable output. However, most of the time the conversation takes off rapidly and barely pauses for breath. If conversation flags, the following questions may be useful:

- What have been the key success factors in this area?

- How was this success achieved?

- If you were doing it all over again, how would you approach it?

- What are the key challenges in this area?

- How have people tackled these challenges?

- Is there anything you wish you had done (with the benefit of hindsight)?

- Any anecdotes or war stories?

- What would be your 3 (5, 10) pieces of advice for other teams/sites?

- *Validation of this knowledge by feeding it back to the main group* – The groups reconvene in the main room and each group feeds back their findings for discussion in the wider group. The feedback sessions can usefully be recorded on audio or video. Also make sure you record the details of the discussion that follows, as much valuable knowledge may be exchanged.

- The next set of dialogue follows, around the next set of issues, until all issues have been discussed.

- Discuss 'how do we continue this exchange when the meeting is over?' The attendees at the knowledge exchange might have developed some close relationships that will form the foundation for a powerful community of practice. The attendees need to agree on the processes for keeping the community alive once the meeting is over. They will need to appoint a coordinator and other roles, choose a communication mechanism, determine a meetings schedule and begin a discussion on aims and objectives and ground rules. They will need to start up a membership list and develop a plan for enrolling other members.

- Closure of the meeting with thanks from senior manager.
- Follow-up to the knowledge exchange (building the community of practice, publishing the knowledge asset – see page 70 for further details on knowledge assets).

A tremendous amount of knowledge is generated at a knowledge exchange. This knowledge needs to be captured and will form the basis for a knowledge asset. Capture the information using audio recording, which can be transcribed, and video recording of feedback sessions or presentations. Get copies of any documents or examples shown at the meeting and take photographs of any flipchart diagrams and of all the attendees.

We worked with one company to facilitate and record a knowledge exchange on 'bidding to win private finance initiative (PFI) contracts'. The purpose of the knowledge exchange was to improve company success by identifying and compiling best practice in PFI bidding. We invited a total of 20 people involved in PFI contracts, either as members of bid teams or as members of teams delivering against PFI contracts, from Europe, the Middle East, New Zealand, Australia and America. Some of the 15 topics under discussion included building the market, knowing the customer, selling the benefits, selecting partners, structuring the bid organisation, the bid process, and negotiation and closing. There was some fantastic dialogue around these issues and we recorded the output as frequently asked questions (FAQs) and video summaries, then created a knowledge asset to summarise the best approaches in winning these bids.

SABMiller used processes similar to knowledge exchange when building their 'Marketing Way'. 'The process of compiling the Marketing Way showed the kind of collaborative learning that the group as a whole is working towards,' they claim. 'Instead of the corporate centre laying down the rules or trying to manage the local marketing process, we took the best ideas and expertise from around the world and distilled them into clear principles, an end-to-end process framework and a set of tools for businesses to apply as appropriate. In this way, each local team retains its autonomy but can benefit from the learning and insight of SABMiller as a whole.'[2]

Another organisation uses a knowledge exchange amongst senior marketers to review the historic results of marketing campaigns in order to draw out generic lessons. These lessons are then used by marketing teams around the world to guide their marketing strategies.

Knowledge market

A knowledge market is like a knowledge exchange, but it is focused on setting up small dialogues, almost mini-peer assists, between the participants, rather than facilitated whole-group discussions. During the early stages of the event or even before the event, you ask each participant to identify three knowledge offers and three knowledge wants:

- *Knowledge offers* – What knowledge do you bring to this? What are the areas within the identified topic where you feel you have a lot of knowledge and experience to offer? These need not be areas where your business has performed well – you may have learned the hard way! Choose three areas where you have knowledge to offer.

- What knowledge do you want to take away? What are the areas where you feel you have a lot to learn? Choose three areas of knowledge where you need knowledge.

People can write their wants and offers on Post-it notes, place them on the wall and begin to group them by themes. Where you can find matching wants and offers under a single theme – in other words where somebody is looking for knowledge that another person can supply – you can set up mini-peer assists to exchange the knowledge there and then. Alternatively, you can schedule follow-up meetings for longer peer assists.

Where there are multiple offers under a single theme – in other words where many people are offering good practice in the same area – you can continue along the lines of a normal knowledge exchange to develop a knowledge asset of current best practice.

Where there are multiple wants under a single theme but no offers – in other words where most of the people are looking for knowledge and guidance in an area – you can set up action learning sets (a process to actively seek new knowledge) or commission research to gain the knowledge.

In Chapter 9, Linda Davies of Mars describes 'Show and Tell' meetings, a type of knowledge market where dialogue sessions are based on 'displays' by various teams, which they use to exhibit a solution they recommend to other teams. These sessions invariably create a huge amount of discussion and it is common for people to leave the meeting with examples from other markets, to implement/use themselves when they get back home.

Retrospect

The retrospect is one of the most effective processes for capturing lessons after the end of a large piece of work. It is a meeting where the team members get together and discuss the history of the activity, the successes and challenges, and identify the learning points for the future. With a retrospect, you can bring out the key knowledge and experience developed by a project team and turn it into actions and resources for the benefit of future teams. By facilitating a dialogue within the whole team, you can highlight the knowledge that comes from the team interactions – knowledge that any one individual may be unaware of, but which the team as a whole knows. Retrospects are commonly used by bid teams at the end of bids or by a marketing team at the end of a marketing campaign or a product launch. One sales organisation calls these meetings 'post-completion analysis meetings'. 'Once a project is completed we'll take a look and say, "Okay, what were the goals? Did we achieve them? How did we do against them? What lessons are there to be learned here? Should we repeat this or should we not?"'

Retrospects are face-to-face meetings that take place as soon as possible after a project or activity is completed. The duration varies depending on the number of people, length and complexity of the project. They can last from 30 minutes to an hour for a short, simple project or four or more hours for a 10-person, six-month duration project. A general rule of thumb for working out how long to allow is to multiply the number of people on the team, or the number who will be attending the retrospect, by 30 minutes.

Retrospect set-up

It is important to schedule the retrospect close to the end of the project, before the team moves on to new work and while memories are fresh. It can be useful to combine the retrospect with an end-of-project celebration and treat it as a close-out exercise for the team. It is important that everybody on the team attends and somebody who was not part of the project team should facilitate the retrospect. The better the facilitator, the better the outcome of the retrospect will be. Find a good facilitator who has a clear idea of the retrospect process and of the purpose of the exercise. Retrospects are not complicated meetings, but they do need attention to purpose, attention to behaviours and, in particular, attention to the quality of the lessons that are identified. Understanding and following the process are key to a successful outcome.

It is very powerful if you can find somebody who will reuse the lessons – perhaps the project leader for the next bid project – and get them to attend the retrospect as an observer. Their presence will give the process a greater level of focus and legitimacy and they can help make sure that the lessons that come out of the retrospect are expressed as useful recommendations and advice. For example, one organisation we worked with had just won a bid for major construction work in a former Soviet country. They invited the bid manager from a neighbouring country to attend their post-bid retrospect. As he was in the process of compiling a bid himself, many of the lessons could be transferred immediately and he was able to probe for useful, specific actionable detail. This knowledge reuser should not facilitate the retrospect; they will have their own agenda, which should not be allowed to dominate the meeting, as they will not be the only users of this knowledge. The facilitator needs to make sure that all the knowledge from the project is captured, not just the knowledge that will be immediately reused in the next project.

The retrospect process is described below:

Introduction

The first step in a retrospect is to set the scene by discussing the purpose of the meeting, the process of the meeting and the ground rules for it. Make it clear that the meeting is held to capture the lessons, in order to help future teams (or the same team in the future). The purpose of the meeting is not to assign blame or to assign praise, but to make life easier for the next project. Also, make it clear what you will do with the output from the meeting, especially if you are recording the event. Once retrospects have become an established standard process, you don't really need to set the scene, but where this is a new process you may need some careful set-up at the beginning of the meeting.

Project objectives

Next you need to review the objectives of the project itself. Ask the project leader to start off this section. If they can find the original terms of reference, this is good because it adds some ground truth and reminds everybody of what they set out to do in the beginning. It is worth reviewing whether these objectives have changed, whether there were any hidden objectives and whether people had any personal goals. No need to ask if these existed. Depending on the scale of the project, this may take between five minutes and 30 minutes to do this.

Project achievements

The next stage involves looking at what actually happened in the project and what was achieved at the end. Again, try to get to the ground truth. What was the actual expenditure compared with the budget? Were the deliverables ready when they were supposed to be? What response was received by the client? What was the uplift in sales? In a long or complicated project, you may need to draw a flowchart of what happened before you can start to analyse it.

Identification of issues

The next stage is the identification of the success factors and challenges that need to be analysed and from which lessons can be drawn. There are a number of ways to do this:

- You can ask people to identify successes and challenges before the event, so you have a shortlist before the retrospect itself. This is effective if you can get the team's attention, but often people do not give it much thought. It may be the only way to identify success factors and challenges from people who cannot attend the event.

- You can ask the attendees to brainstorm their top three (for example) success factors and top three challenges and put them on individual Post-it notes, which can then be grouped into themes for analysis.

- You can map out the flow of the project, including the major tasks, activities and steps and then ask people to identify the activities that were particularly successful or challenging. Prioritise these areas for further discussion and analysis.

- Ask people in turn to identify their successes and then prioritise them. This method is difficult to facilitate as people will start discussing the items rather than just identifying them.

- Ask people in turn to identify their successes and discuss them in the group as each one is identified. This method ensures that everybody contributes, but it may be difficult to manage the time.

Discussion of issues and identification of learning points

Take the issues one by one, in order of priority, and hold a group dialogue on each one to find the root causes of the success ('Everybody, why do you think this was successful? What did you do to ensure success?'); and continue the dialogue to ask how the success can be repeated in future ('So what would you recommend to a team doing this in future, to repeat the success? If you were doing it again tomorrow, what would you put in place?'). I like to discuss the success factors in order of priority first and then discuss the challenges in order of priority. This section of the retrospect can take between 10 and 20 minutes for each person present (so if six people are present, it could take between one and two hours). The purpose of the discussion is to come up with good-quality lessons, namely specific, useful, actionable recommendations for future projects, which will allow them to reproduce the identified success. Good, firm facilitation may be needed here, otherwise the meeting can easily lapse into a discussion of what people liked about the project (or worse, into a blamestorming session) or can generate woolly and vague lessons. With firm facilitation, some very useful material can be developed for future teams.

During this process you may also identify procedures, documents or other artefacts that may be useful for future projects or teams. For example, if a success factor was the clear definition of roles at the start of bid preparation, you can ask for a copy of the role definition document, which can then be reused by future bid teams as a template or a starter for their own role definition document.

Occasionally, when reviewing a difficult project, conflict may arise. Different people at the retrospect may have different perceptions of what happened to cause a breakdown or failure in the project. Arguments can start, tempers can rise. The way to turn conflict into a positive outcome is to ask the question, 'what should we do *next time*, in future projects, to ensure this breakdown or failure does not happen again?' In many ways it does not matter precisely what happened this time or whose fault it was, so long as everybody is agreed on how to do it better next time. In fact, the question 'what should we do next time?' is the most powerful question to ask in retrospects. It is almost worth writing this question on a flipchart and sticking it on the wall. The whole purpose of the retrospect is finding lessons that can be reapplied next time or in the next project.

Offers for the next project

A further step can be to ask the project team what they can provide for the next project to help them perform. Obviously they can give them the results of the retrospect, but they may be able to offer them documentation, advice, templates, campaign material and boilerplate bid text.

Closure

As a closure exercise, at the end of the retrospect, I like to go round the room and ask people to rate their satisfaction with the project, as 'marks out of 10'. Sometimes, if the project has delivered a great result through struggle and hardship, I ask them to rate their satisfaction first with the product they delivered and second, with the process they went through. This satisfaction rating exercise has three main purposes:

- It allows people to express their feelings about the project without having to use emotional words. Given that they have been reliving the project during the course of the retrospect, discussing the highs and lows, it is quite good to 'even out' with an overview statement of how they feel.

- It allows you to identify the outliers. If everybody was giving the project 8 out of 10, apart from one person who gave it 2 out of 10, then you need to understand why.

- It allows you to ask a supplementary question: What was missing from the project that would have allowed you to give it 10 out of 10?

Recording retrospects

Knowledge has credibility when it is expressed by credible people – people with experience. Knowledge captured in the form of quotes or soundbites from the project team can be seen as being the voice of experience and can be used in stories to add context to the identified lessons. If you are going to add context and credibility in this way, the retrospect needs to be recorded carefully – recording people's own words as closely as possible, recording the stories that give context to the lessons and recording who said what. You either have to take very detailed notes (speed-writing) or, if possible, you should audio-record the event. Although some people may worry about having a tape recorder present, you can reassure them that it is only for transcription purposes, that any recordings will be destroyed after transcription and that nothing will be published without giving the retrospect attendees the opportunity to edit it first. However, the amount of learning that emerges during a retrospect is so huge that often audio-recording is the only practical way to capture it all.

It can also be useful to summarise some of the key retrospect lessons and stories on video. At the end of the retrospect, when the lessons have been identified and discussed, ask a few of the more eloquent speakers to summarise what has been learned and what they would recommend to future projects based on that learning. These small video summaries can be a good and engaging way of recording some of the key lessons. They are frequently stored as part of the knowledge asset on the topic.

Retrospects (with some individual interviews) were the tool of choice for one organisation that we worked with to collect and collate their knowledge on 'winning work'. This was compiled from the knowledge of their bid teams and covered elements such as business development, partnering, prequalification, building the bid team, bid preparation, document preparation, pricing, customer relationships and negotiation. It is no surprise that many of these themes are the same as those from the PFI knowledge exchange described above, as these are part of the standard steps of preparing any bid and elements that each bidding organisation has to perfect.

Mini-knowledge exchange and peer assist at team meetings

The sections above describe knowledge exchange and peer assist as specific events held for members of a community of practice or members of a single discipline to exchange knowledge about a topic. However, knowledge exchange can also take place on a much smaller scale and with much less formality, during normal meetings. For example, members of a dispersed regional sales team, working individually most of the time, will frequently get together for team meetings on a weekly or even monthly basis. This is a good opportunity to share knowledge with each other, ask for help and advice and share best practice.

The manager of such a team needs to set not only the culture that allows such exchange of knowledge, but also the expectations, and to provide a structure that ensures exchange of knowledge. The following quotes are from a survey we ran of sales managers and sales reps. They do not only show the value of exchanging knowledge in team meetings and team conference calls, but also reflect the influence of the manager in driving this behaviour.

We are each other's only resource. Somebody will figure something out when they're doing their work and then, whenever it comes up as a question for somebody else, we all just have to work together and share our learnings and pass it on, to speed things along on the learning curve. Our boss doesn't know our system as well as we do and we can teach each other. Whenever we have questions, we usually go to each other before we take it anywhere else.

There's a lot of sharing that goes on within the team and before that we were pretty much just silos. There's probably something that comes out of every meeting where someone is saying, 'Does anybody know how I can get past this roadblock?' or 'Is there something that I could do to help facilitate this?' And there's been a lot of times where someone else on the team said, 'Here's how I've been able to accomplish that.' Or 'Have you thought about talking to this person in this department?' It'll be surfaced at the team meeting if somebody is having an issue with something and most of the time somebody within the team can propose a solution.

You need to take all of these opportunities and make them learning opportunities to try to make the team better. Really look for best practices. It's not just 'Look at that (sales) number, you're down, you're here, you're whatever.' It's 'Hey Jim, it looks as though you were at 125 a year ago, what do you attribute your success to? Why do you think you're doing so well?' And do that in a group conversation. And then if somebody's down, 'What are the issues that you are facing right now? Is there anything that we can help you with?' On paper it looks like this guy isn't pulling their own weight. But in the meanwhile they may be pulling their weight, once you understand exactly what the root problem is.

(Our sales manager) is always looking for successes that one person has and trying to find ways that those successes can be transferred to other accounts. He doesn't just go into one area and say, 'Well, so and so did this and I want you to try it,' instead, he's really good at facilitating the communication between the various field managers so that they're sharing the successes and working on solutions together for each other's accounts.

Don't be afraid to ask your peers questions (in these meetings). 'I'm a new account manager, new to the channel or new to the business,' don't be afraid to ask questions. Pick the brains of the sales reps that are currently on the team.

When you identify some of the key learnings someone else on the team will say, 'Hey, you know what, I had that same experience, this is what I did which was better and different and you should try that approach'. Or, 'Hey, have you tried to ask so-and-so in the national office for resources to help get that project completed?' So you review it as a team, you talk about the key learnings, you talk about some shortfalls or the misses, then you know other people can share experiences and it literally will help that person or will help the entire team.

I think it's great because I worked previously in a world basically where I was kind of out on my own in a very unique group and so did not have a lot of that sharing that took place amongst my fellow peers. And coming to this new group, it is quite the opposite. We have this information and it flows freely and I just think it's great because you can feel comfortable saying, 'I have to work on a presentation coming up; I'm getting ready for this certain project, does anybody have anything that may help me here?' And people send information; I think that's a very positive thing about our team.

These seven quotes from different teams show the sort of informal knowledge-sharing that can be promoted within a sales team. It is the manager's job to build this open culture, where people are willing to share lessons and ask each other for advice (for more details see Chapter 8). Some useful questions the manager can ask in a team meeting to promote this behaviour are:

- 'Susie, you've had a very successful month, can you share with us what you did and what you can recommend to others?'
- 'John has some big challenges on his account. Can anybody think of things that he could do to turn the situation around?'
- 'Guys, it looks like we are all facing a challenge on this particular brand, can we put our heads together and pool what we know to decide the best way to tackle it?'

After action review (AAR)

After action reviews (AARs) are short conversations about learning, which can be conducted on a regular basis. They allow a team or individual to consciously express what they've learned, for others to hear this and learn from it and for teams to change and improve their processes depending on what's been learned. AARs are particularly suited to the sales and marketing environment as they are simple to conduct and have immediate benefit. They could for example be routinely used to capture what has happened during a sales visit, by conducting them immediately after the visit, often in a coffee shop or sitting in a car in the client's car park. In many ways AARs can be thought of as 'learning how we performed today so we can perform better tomorrow'.

The AAR process was developed by the US Army, which uses it as their main knowledge-gathering process. It does not go into very great analytical depth and so is useful for reviewing short-turnaround activity or single actions. It is short and focused enough to do on a weekly or daily basis, perhaps during weekly team meetings. As one sales team reports, 'On our conference calls we'll go over the numbers and spend some time talking about what drove the numbers. Why did we have the successes that we did, why do we have the disappointments, what are we going to do differently in the new year?'

The structure of an AAR is very simple. It consists of asking five questions – the five listed below. The questions are answered through dialogue within the team:

- *What was supposed to happen?* The first question is asked about the objective of the activity and the target performance. We have often found that the first few times you ask this question, people may turn out to have been confused about the objective or the target or else no clear objective was set. One of the by-products of AARs is that they promote objective-setting.

- *What actually happened?* The second question looks at actual performance. If you are conducting an AAR, you need to establish 'ground truth' with this question. You are looking to determine reality, rather than opinion. This is where you have to ensure that you avoid opinion and emotion. It is very easy for the discussion to become heated at this point. Try to avoid that by always coming back to 'ground truth' – what actually happened and what is the evidence to support it (sales figures, for example, or customer comments)?

- *Why was there a difference?* The third question seeks to understand why a particular result was achieved. Perhaps you did better than expected; perhaps you did worse than expected; perhaps you met your target. What were the factors that determined the result? Another way to ask this question, if the first way doesn't work, is *'What went well and what did not go so well?'*

- *What have we learned?* The fourth question asks about the learning and should be expressed in terms of what will be done differently in future (or, in cases of over-performance, what should be repeated in future).

- *What action needs to be taken?* Here you move from analysis of the activity to 'what are we going to do about it?' Now you need to assign the action to ensure it gets done. Much of the time the action lies with the team. If the team cannot fix the action, there needs to be an escalation route.

In many textbooks the AAR process is illustrated by using four questions. We prefer five to highlight the move from lesson identification to lesson learned.

The answers to these questions can usefully be recorded on a one-page *pro forma* or a marked-up flipchart, which can be collected for future reference.

The after action review process works well in an open, blame-free, inclusive environment. You need to set the ground rules for after-action reviews, and some of the rules are as follows:

- Aim for openness, not hiding any mistakes.

- There should be no hierarchy – everyone's input is equally valid.

- The focus of the exercise is learning, not blame or evaluation.

- Everyone who was involved in the activity should take part in the AAR.

- No outsiders should be present; nobody should be there to 'audit performance'.

- Deal with the significant issues and the significant objectives, not trivia.

One organisation that made powerful use of after action review in sales was Buckman Laboratories. As M. Sheldon Ellis and Melissie Rumizen tell us:[3]

> The After Action Review met most of our standards for business processes. Additionally, it was a natural companion to another

business process for planning. However, it failed to meet our requirement for a visual representation. So we created our own, one that in the words of our Manager of Instructional Design, Catherine Walker, 'can be drawn in the dust on the hood of a sales associate's pick-up truck'. With our adaptation of the AAR, we 'Buckmanized' it by naming it the Buckman After Action Review (BAAR). Overall, since the inception of our knowledge sharing system,[4] we've experienced a 50 percent rise in sales from new products, which indicates a dramatic rise in profitability from innovation. Sales per associate have increased 51 percent, while operating profit per associate has gone up 93 percent. The payoff is clear.

Training, coaching and mentoring

Training, coaching and mentoring also play a role in transferring knowledge, particularly within a team of sales staff who work alone much of the time. The training needs to be personalised to the skills needs of the individual, and the ideal approach is to provide just-in-time training.

One sales manager we interviewed creates individual personalised training programmes for each team member, taking into account their personal motivation, their competences, where they want to develop and how they want to organise their learning. He draws up a training programme with them, helps with the programme and has regular sessions with them to monitor their progress. Some of the training might be preparing in advance for a meeting with the customer, for example, so the salesperson knows what to do, and then afterwards the manager will discuss how the meeting went and so prepare the salesperson for the future. This way, he provides a combination of just-in-time training and ongoing coaching.

When a manager provides the coaching, he can also act as a conduit for learning within the team. As one salesperson reported, 'Our manager makes a point of visiting everybody on the team and spending individual time with them. Those lessons are shared with the group when we are all together – "this is what this person did and it worked, try it, think about how it will fit". And vice versa.'

Coaching is a key managerial skill and a skill that can be learned by the manager. Part of the skill lies in drawing the answers out of the staff, rather than giving them the answers yourself. According to one regional sales manager,

> They might come to me and say 'I am not sure what to do.' Instead of giving the answer, I get them talking. 'Well, tell me what *could* you do?' And then we talk about it and they might realise they have already got the answer. Often my role is to give them the confidence in their own answer. I might say, 'You know this account far better than I, what is your gut feel?' Of course this depends on the situation and if somebody came to me in their first week and I started giving them coaching, we would be there all day!

The manager can also link up experienced sales people with younger inexperienced staff and ask them to act as mentors, to keep an eye on them and to reach out to them on a regular basis to talk about issues, problems and opportunities. Then if the young and inexperienced person has a question or a problem, they feel that there's always somebody there who can help them and someone who is open to answering even the 'dumb questions'. Sales people are often gregarious and many welcome this mentoring role. One of the coaches explained to us, 'I like being able to help someone through a difficult phase in their career or something like that, walking them through it, training them on the tools. That makes me feel good that I've helped somebody else.'

Role-play can be a very powerful training tool for sales staff. For instance, you might train sales people by having two people act out a sale between the buyer and the sales representative. The manager and/or other trainees watch the role-play and debrief it afterwards. Then you can draw out any generic learnings from the role-play (perhaps using the after action review as a framework for debriefing), as well as identifying strengths and areas for development for individual staff. Then you can replay the session, incorporating the learnings. Let the staff experience the changes and the improvement, instead of just imagining what might happen. The use of role-play will vary from one company to another; in some companies it is viewed as 'staged and artificial' while in others it is a vital training tool.

Interviews

An interview is the most effective way to identify lessons from a single person, for example from a key account manager, your most successful marketing manager or your best sales staff. One sales company regularly conducts interviews with their top sales managers to identify their secrets of success, which are then compiled into a knowledge asset. Mars use interviews with staff around the world on strategic topics identified by the community steering team, such as selling to global supermarket chains or understanding the 'impulse buyer' (see Chapter 9 for more details). Interviewing is a skill that can be learned and developed through practice. A structure for interviewing is presented below. It can either be used as a checklist to verify that the trained facilitator/interviewer whom you have engaged to conduct the interview has a process that they will follow, or as an introductory guide to allow you to conduct the interview.

Preparation

Careful preparation will help you and the interviewee and will give a better end product. Allow at least an hour for a normal interview or several hours for an in-depth interview with a senior person such as a sales director or marketing vice president. Make sure the interviewee knows why you are interviewing them, who you are, what the process of the interview will be, how long it will take and what you will do with the output. Make sure you know who they are, why they are important and what their role was in the activity being reviewed. Do a bit of background reading so you understand some of the context and know some of the technical terms.

Explain the process

Be clear about the topic, purpose and ground rules of the interview. You are interviewing this person to identify their lessons, rather than to critique their performance or obtain a magazine article. You therefore need to make it clear to them at the start precisely what you are interviewing them about. For example, 'I would like to interview you for about an hour on what you have learned about sharing knowledge in a dispersed sales team.' You then need to explain what will happen to the output, who will write it up as lessons, what their role is in validating the lessons and how the lessons will be carried through into action. For example, 'The purpose of this exercise is to help sales managers deliver the same degree of success as yours, by building on what you have learned. I will write up the lessons, ask you to review them in about a week's time, and when you have approved them they will be passed to the senior sales directors, who will create some guidelines for the organisation.'

You will also need to explain the process that you will use, ask permission to record and reassure the interviewee that they will have the right to edit the output before it is published. We generally assure the interviewee that any recording (with the exception of video clips) will be for transcription purposes only and ask them to be as open as they like during the interview in the knowledge that they can go back and reword things later. Make sure they realise that their lessons will be attributed to them. These will not be anonymous lessons; the interviewee will be given full credit for their knowledge.

The interview process

During this process you will be helping the interviewee uncover the key bits of knowledge that they may not even realise they have (the unknown knowns). You as interviewer have dual responsibility – first to the interviewee (to help them become aware of what they have learned) and second to the ultimate audience (by making sure that the lessons you help the interviewee to identify will be specific, relevant and actionable). You must ask questions on behalf of the audience and manage the conversation so that useful answers emerge. You are looking for the secrets of this person's success, what they have learned from their experiences and how others can repeat the success. You don't know what these secrets are and the interviewee may not fully know either. So there is no point going into the interview with a list of questions and expecting simple answers – the questioning process is a process of exploration.

Keeping track of the structure

You need to keep good notes in order to follow the questioning structure. When I am conducting an interview, every time the interviewee mentions a new theme, success factor or challenge that will become a new 'branch' in the interview 'tree', I put a big asterisk against it in my notes. Then I can keep checking back and making sure all of these branches have been explored. For example, 'Mr X, earlier you said that team learning had gone well – can we just explore that for a bit? *Why* do you think the teamwork was so good?'

Use your listening skills. Your role is to ask short questions to allow the interviewee to express what he knows. Make sure your listening/speaking ratio is 80:20 or greater. Listening is not passive, however. You need to use 'listening skills'. Some of the basic listening skills include:

- suspending judgement (not trying to analyse if what is being said is right or wrong or whether you agree with it);
- not interrupting (especially when you are recording the interview);
- paraphrasing (i.e. repeating back what someone has said to you using your own words and context, to check for understanding); and
- purpose-stating (saying why you are asking the question).

You need to keep the interview on track by finding a 'nice way' to move them on when they are rambling or going off track. If this happens you might need to ask them, 'So what are the learnings?' to bring them back to the topic being discussed.

Summing up

Once you have explored all the topics and identified all the lessons, a good way to sum up the interview is to ask the interviewee to summarise the top three or top five lessons. The following question is one that we find very useful in prompting a good summary:

> *As a summary of what we have been discussing (and this will probably be repeating some of the things we've been through), if you were speaking to somebody who was just about to start on a similar activity tomorrow, what would your key points of advice be?*

This section of the interview can be a good one to capture on video or audio file. You may want to give them a couple of minutes' preparation or thinking time before running the cameras.

Identifying the documents

As you go through the interview, make a note of any key documents that the interviewee mentions (for example, 'Bill took photographs of the product displays, which we found very useful'). Ask whether you may have an electronic copy of these to include in the final product ('Can you get me a copy of Bill's photographs?'). Again, as you make notes during the interview, you can put a mark against your notes whenever a key document is mentioned. This allows you to refer back to them again at the end ('You mentioned the following key documents – X, Y and Z – do you think you would be able to e-mail these to me by the end of the week?'). These documents may be very useful to attach to the lesson.

Recording

A vast amount of knowledge will come out from an interview. They are a rich source of guidance, anecdote, experience, advice and story and you need to capture this material in an equally rich way. You really need a complete verbatim transcript from which to work. You therefore should record the interview with a digital voice recorder. A simple pocket dictation machine will be sufficient and can sit fairly unobtrusively in front of the interviewee. Make sure whatever recording machine you use is compatible with the transcription service you will employ. Make sure the batteries are fresh and that you have spares. Ideally have a spare recorder. I was interviewing earlier this year and managed to tip a cup of tea over my digital recorder. However, I was prepared and I had a second recorder in my bag.

Take detailed notes as well. Speed-written notes are useful in two ways; as a non-technical backup to the recording equipment and also as a way for you to follow the structure of the interview as it branches. Detailed notes are also valuable as a backup if your recording equipment fails or if the recording is of poor quality. Speed-writing is a useful skill for the knowledge manager, but it is a tiring process. Make sure you have a large notebook and several sharp HB or B pencils. Buy a new notebook for each series of interviews.

It may be useful to take a photograph of the interviewee. Some organisations put the originator's photograph in the lesson document.

Telephone interviews

Sometimes it will just be impossible to conduct the interview face to face, for example if you are interviewing the members of a global team. You will then need to interview them by telephone. The process will be the same, but a telephone interview will require far more concentration than face to face. You may also need to spend additional time setting up the context and establishing rapport. It is not so easy to 'break the ice' in a telephone interview and you will need to go quite carefully through who you are, who commissioned the lessons identification and what you will do with the output. As you conduct the remote interview, be careful to explain what you're doing in more detail than you would face to face. For example, 'I would like to ask one or two context-setting questions and then we will go into more detail,' or 'Can I please follow up on that point, because I think this would be a very useful area to discuss further?'

Take care with recording. Often the best you can do is to place a tape recorder next to a speaker phone or video-conference loudspeaker. It is better to buy a splitter that takes an audio stream from a telephone handset socket. You should use a speakerphone or a telephone headset, so you have both your hands free for taking notes. Do not audio-tape a telephone conversation without the person at the other end being aware beforehand that you are going to tape the conversation.

Knowledge asset

The output from multiple interviews, from retrospects or from a knowledge exchange can be built into a knowledge asset. Knowledge assets consist of guidelines, set within a business context, enlivened by stories and quotes from experience and linked to people and documents for further investigation. The role of knowledge assets in knowledge management is to provide the means by which one team or person can transfer their know-how to many teams or people, separated in time and distance. Although the most effective mechanism for knowledge transfer is face to face, this is not always possible to arrange. Your knowledge management system should provide the means to transfer knowledge between people, even if the timespan between capture and use is years. A knowledge asset can usefully be hosted on a wiki or in a knowledge base.

Setting the context

You need to be very clear about the purpose of the knowledge asset and also who the user of the knowledge asset will be. The user will often help define the scope and purpose. Once you have purpose, scope and user, you need to make sure you have the resources needed to complete the exercise.

Capturing the knowledge

Processes for capturing knowledge have already been described in this chapter; they include after-action review, retrospect and individual interviews.

Distilling out the lessons

The analysis and distillation step consists of looking back at what happened and turning this into forward-looking advice for the future. Lessons can be presented as recommendations for the future or as questions that future users should ask themselves or, in the simplest case, as a checklist for future users to follow. Use the transcripts from the knowledge capture process to derive quotes that answer the questions (or illustrate the recommendations), which can then be grouped into themes. During a long knowledge capture process involving many people, analysis can be run in parallel with the later interviews.

Validating the lessons

Any lessons, recommendations or questions/answers derived during the distillation phase need to be validated with the team and with the wider community of practice.

Setting out the contents of the knowledge asset

A knowledge asset can be built from the experiences of a single project team or by collating know-how and experience from many teams. The contents of a knowledge asset may include some or all of the following:

- a history of the activity or projects (if the knowledge asset is compiled from project activity);

- guidance for future teams, based on the experience of the people who contributed to the knowledge asset, illustrated with verbatim attributed quotes. This guidance could be in the form of frequently asked questions or checklists or guidelines;

- contact details of the people who contributed to the knowledge asset;
- links to documents and other artefacts that future teams will find useful;
- metadata (data about the knowledge asset, such as author, date, etc.).

Choice of media

Different people learn in different ways and the richer the medium, the more easily knowledge is transferred. Although your knowledge asset will probably be text-based (unless you are creating a video), you should consider including pictures, audio and/or video, depending on your available bandwidth and technology. Multimedia wikis have huge value as a medium for storing a knowledge asset, as it can so easily be updated as new knowledge becomes available. Knowledge goes out of date if it is not kept fresh.

Publishing the knowledge asset

The knowledge asset needs to be placed somewhere that knowledge customers can find it in the future. Publish it in 'community space' and let the community of practice know that it has been published. The advantage of publishing it on a community wiki is that community members can then edit the asset further. Seek feedback on your knowledge asset, appoint a knowledge owner for the asset and make sure the asset is updated regularly.

Some of the knowledge assets that we have helped to create for sales and marketing organisations include the following topics (many of them mentioned above), which give some idea of the range of topics suitable for knowledge assets:

- winning work;
- bidding for PFI contracts;
- building an engaged sales workforce;
- marketing to the impulse buyer;
- selling to major accounts;
- partnering along the supply chain.

Best practice

The concept of 'best practice' is a contentious one in knowledge management circles. In the discussion groups, we hear people saying, 'We don't believe in best practice.' Respected KM gurus say that 'best practice harms effectiveness'. David Snowden, in his complexity model, believes that best practice will apply only to simple, repeatable, non-complex problems. Certainly we have seen the concept of best practice used negatively and destructively in organisations. People can defend outmoded and inefficient ways of working by saying 'we are following best practice' or can force a solution on an inappropriate problem by saying 'it must work – it's best practice'. However, the allure of 'best practice' is strong and many companies aspire to developing and deploying best practices in a number of sales and marketing areas.

We believe that best practice is a very useful concept, provided you follow the rules below:

1. Best is temporary. There may be a current 'best way' to do something, but like 'world champion' or 'world record', it's not going to stay the best for long.

2. Best is therefore a starting point. You should always look to improve on best, but without knowing the temporary best, you don't know what you have to beat. Like a world record, best is there to be beaten – it's a minimum accepted threshold.

3. Best is contextual. There may be no universal 'best way' to do something. The best way to market hair dye in Norway may not be the best way to market hair dye in Nigeria. However, in each context there will be a best practice; for example, a Scandinavian best practice, a West African best practice, etc.

4. In a new context, you cannot blindly apply 'best' from another context. However, you can learn from other 'bests' – no context is ever totally alien and there may be approaches that you can reuse and approaches you can use to inform your own approach.

5. Best practice does not have to be written down. It can live there in the community cloud of tacit knowledge. Usain Bolt's 'best way to run a sprint' is probably not even conscious – it's in his muscle memory. However, if it can be written down – in a wiki or a document or a knowledge asset – so much the better, so long as it is immediately updated every time it's superseded and improved. The risk with documenting a best practice is that it goes out of date and there is no

point in documenting without allowing for continual update. The risk with not documenting a best practice is that people can't find it, can't refer to it and so make up their own practice, which is frequently far from best. The answer is to record and continually update – through a wiki or through a constantly reviewed and updated knowledge asset.

If you apply these five caveats, there is little or no risk from the concept of best practice and instead it can be part of the engine that drives continual improvement. After all, the concept of best practice is simply the following thought process: 'Here's a problem. Has anyone seen anything like this before? What's the best way they've found to deal with things like this? How can I build on/improve on that to tackle my problem? Hmm – that worked, I'd better let others know what I did.'

Best practices are a particularly valuable concept in organisations with global brands and a level of commonality between the different countries. Proctor & Gamble, for example, claim that their scale advantage is driven as much by knowledge-sharing, common systems and processes and best practices as it is by size and scope.[5] Many organisations seek to develop internal best practices or 'standard ways of working' in areas such as sales and marketing and we have already mentioned the SABMiller Marketing Way. In their 2009 Annual Report, SABMiller describe the value of applying their Marketing Way in Colombia:

> Colombia's Pony Malta is a category-leading, non-alcoholic, malt beverage competing directly with carbonated soft drinks, juices and dairy beverages. Following the principles of SABMiller's Marketing Way, the Colombian business continued the brand's evolution in 2008 by positioning the product as a 'natural balance between nutrition and refreshment'. The challenge, then, was to differentiate the brand from rival categories while appealing to audiences with different priorities – children and young people who mainly drink it for refreshment and their mothers who value its nutritional properties.
>
> The resulting campaign mixed traditional advertising with point-of-sale merchandising, prize giveaways and multi-media promotions. Initiatives included the 'Pony Futbol' event involving more than 25,000 young footballers around the country. In the year to 31 March 2009, the brand increased its sales volumes by 3.4%. Having consolidated its position as number two in Colombia's carbonated soft drink category, after Coca-Cola, Pony Malta is well placed to continue growing.

Best practices such as the Marketing Way need to be gathered through knowledge exchanges and interviews, fully described in a knowledge asset, owned by a knowledge owner (Chapter 6), spread throughout a community of practice (Chapter 4) and kept alive and up to date.

Storytelling and case histories

Even the clearest knowledge benefits from being illustrated with a story. The learning has been identified within a context and it helps to understand the context when reviewing the learning, so that the user can know whether it applies to them. Therefore a story can support a learning point through providing valuable background and context. Listening to a story is also a more natural way of learning than reading a piece of text. A story can include inflection and stress and emotion that otherwise is lacking. There is therefore a considerable amount of interest in storytelling in knowledge management circles and stories need to be included in knowledge assets to provide context, emotion and a human link.

Stories used for transferring knowledge need certain characteristics:

- *They need to be true* – There is no value in a made-up story; people will find out that it is not true and then you lose all credibility. Knowledge can be transferred through stories, if they are true.

- *They need to be told by the people concerned* – Stories lose their power when they come second-hand. They need to come from someone involved or someone with direct contact with the people involved. Obviously these people can't be everywhere; they can't go round telling their story to everyone, so record them on video. *New Scientist* magazine recently reported on a study in Benin, in the *International Journal of Agricultural Sustainability*. The study described how a team from the West Africa Rice Centre was attempting to transfer knowledge to women farmers in West Africa, on the topic of 'how to parboil rice'. They tried a variety of ways to transfer the knowledge, including workshop demonstrations and video demonstrations. They found that firstly the video attracted more watchers than the conventional workshops (74 per cent of women in the villages, as opposed to 22 per cent) and secondly that the reuse of the knowledge by those who attended was much higher (72 per cent as opposed to 19 per cent). This was at least partly because the people telling the story in the video were women rice farmers from Africa, not Western scientists. This delivered a level of trust in the knowledge, as it was being demonstrated by peers and by the people concerned with rice preparation.

- *They need a clear learning point* – Not every form of storytelling is effective for sharing knowledge. We can tell stories for many reasons, such as interest and entertainment and scandal, without necessarily deriving lessons from them or sharing knowledge through them. Storytelling alone, with no learning points, is not an efficient way of learning and even a story that conveys learning benefits from clear identification of the learning and the recommendations arising. Without this, everybody listening to the story would need to draw their own conclusion. For experienced staff, this may be all right, but inexperienced staff may miss the learning points completely or draw the wrong conclusion. The most qualified person to draw the conclusion is the one who lived through the story. Why not let him or her share their conclusion as something that others can learn from? Stories are easiest to learn from when they carry a learning point that others can use to guide their action.

If you are capturing stories as part of your knowledge management programme, a digital video camera is a key part of your toolkit. When the camera is being used to create video clips for use in PowerPoint presentations or on your intranet, it doesn't matter whether you choose a camera that records onto disc or one that records onto cassettes or onto flash memory, as the quality will be much the same when it is shrunk to broadcast size. We currently prefer flash memory for ease of file transfer.

Look for a camera that takes an external microphone. This is important! People will put up with a poor picture in a video, rather than poor sound. Modern digital video cameras have built-in microphones that are incredibly sensitive and can pick up noise from the cassette, from the spinning disc or from background noise such as air-conditioning or road noise. It is far better to use an external tie-clip microphone that you can attach to the person telling the story, so that the sound is as clear as possible. Then you need to invest in video editing software. There are many choices and all seem pretty good if your only aim is to record stories.

Notes

1. Milton, Nick (2010) *The Lessons Learned Handbook*. Oxford: Chandos Publishing.

2. *http://www.sabmiller.com/files/reports/ar2008/6_strategic/priority4.html*
3. M. Sheldon Ellis and Melissie Rumizen (2002) 'The evolution of KM at Buckman Laboratories: How its KM program has developed with the new leadership', *KM Review*, Vol 5, Issue 1, March/April.
4. This includes far more than just the BAAR.
5. *http://annualreport.pg.com/annualreport2009/letter/strength.shtml*

Communities in sales and marketing

Communities have a huge role to play in knowledge management in the sales and marketing areas. As we describe this role, we will discuss three different types of communities: communities of practice, communities of purpose and communities of interest.

- **Communities of practice** are the knowledge management standard. A community of practice is, as you might expect, a community of practitioners – practitioners within a single area or discipline. They may be a community of sales people, a community of marketers, a technical support community or a bid community. Their conversation is about practice – about selling, about marketing, about bidding – and the purpose of the community is primarily to help each other to improve their practice, by using the tacit knowledge of the community as a shared resource. By sharing what they know, they become better sellers, better marketers, etc. The community does not deliver anything collectively to their host company; all the output they create is for the benefit of the community members. Communities of practice generally are voluntary and often have little or no funding from the host company.

- **Communities of purpose** are different. They are funded by a company or by a host organisation and, in return, commit to deliverables. This type of community will have an identified set of members, rather than being totally voluntary. They will have joint objectives. They often act as a virtual team. Their conversation is about practice, so they are different from a multi-discipline team, but in many ways they behave like a team. An example of these communities of purpose is the global practice groups at Mars, described in Chapter 9.

- **Communities of interest** are different again. These consist of people who are interested in a particular topic, but it is not their area of practice. Their purpose is to receive and share information, but this

Figure 4.1 The three community types

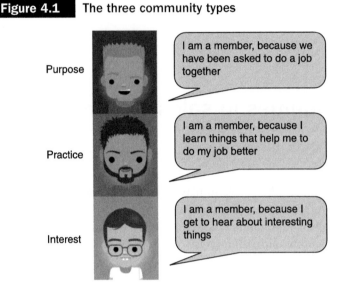

Purpose — I am a member, because we have been asked to do a job together

Practice — I am a member, because I learn things that help me to do my job better

Interest — I am a member, because I get to hear about interesting things

information is not about their practice area. Membership is entirely voluntary. In the sales and marketing world, these communities might be external customer communities or internal product communities for sharing product information along the supply chain. There has been a lot of interest recently in building communities of interest among the customer base using social networking software, as a way of building brand loyalty.

We will look at these three types of community in more detail below.

Communities of practice

Communities of practice are peer networks of practitioners within an organisation that help each other perform better by sharing lessons and knowledge. Many large companies have set up dozens of communities of practice, some of which may have over a thousand members. Communities generally have a facilitator or moderator and may sometimes have a sophisticated governance system. Community members exchange knowledge in two ways. They can capture, create and/or share process documents or they can use discussion forums to ask each other for help and advice.

For a community of practice to operate effectively as a mechanism for sharing knowledge, it needs the following enablers:

A way to ask questions and give answers

The primary way for community members to access the tacit knowledge of the organisation is through asking questions. Any community member facing a problem where they lack complete knowledge should have a means of asking the community for help and of receiving answers. In a co-located community, this can be done in regular face-to-face meetings. Communities of practice in dispersed or multinational businesses cannot meet regularly face to face. They need some virtual means of raising questions and receiving answers.

There are many web-based or e-mail-based discussion tools or question and answer forum tools that allow just this facility, and these are proven and popular tools for sharing knowledge within communities. Buckman Laboratories, for example, operate several global communities of practice, each with its own online Q&A forum, so that customer-facing sales agents anywhere in the world can access lessons from their peers by sending an e-mail asking for lessons and advice. An e-mail will be forwarded to all members of the community and anybody who can share their learning will reply. Replies are collated as a 'threaded discussion' on a community forum and community members can read this discussion and their own comments and learn themselves. Social networking software such as Facebook, Twitter, Yammer and SalesForce Chatter also allows community members to ask each other for help and advice.

This sort of online interaction has historically worked better for marketing than for sales, as marketers are more likely to be sitting behind a desk and in front of a screen. However, the increase in power and connectivity of handheld tools and smartphones now means that sales people can join in the online conversation from anywhere they happen to be. This is discussed further in Chapter 6.

A sense of identity

The members of a community are happy to share lessons with each other because they feel a sense of identity with each other. They see each other as fellow practitioners, sharing the same challenges, facing the same issues and having valuable learning to share. People will feel 'at home' in a community if they identify with the community topic. Therefore the most effective communities tend to be the ones that deal with people's core tasks. When you get a group of sales reps in a bar, they tend to talk sales all night. This is the sort of interest, energy and identification with the topic that will really hold a community together. The sense of identity can be strengthened through a face-to-face community launch meeting and then regular face-to-face meetings of the community and by focusing the community on core jobs. So if your sales force is split by product category, such as sellers of cosmetics, sellers of health foods, sellers of medicines, it makes sense to have three communities of practice: Cosmetics Sales, Health Sales, Medical Sales. If, however, the same sales team is responsible for all three categories of product, just have a single sales community. As described in Chapter 9, the marketing communities at Mars are based on global brands and on issues such as marketing petcare products in the developing world, while the sales communities are cross-product-segment communities related to sales, such as selling through distributors or selling to global supermarket chains.

An energetic coordinator

The community of practice needs a defined coordinator.[1] This is the person who is accountable for the smooth operation of the community. Some of the responsibilities of the coordinator include:

- managing the community discussions (online and face to face);
- making sure agreed community behaviours are followed;
- setting up the community meetings;
- working with the community core team;
- liaising with subject matter experts and process owners;
- watching for problems where knowledge-sharing is not happening;
- maintaining the membership list;
- representing the community to management;
- managing the lifecycle of the community;
- keeping energy levels high amongst participants, to ensure active participation.

The most important attributes for the community coordinator are passion and energy. The coordinator of the community acts as the dynamo for the community, keeping energy levels high and positive. The community coordinator needs to be an insider; they need to be a member of the organisation, they need to be well known and well respected and they need to be a practitioner in the topic. They have to understand the jargon and the language and they have to know the key players. The community leaders can be appointed (as in Buckman Laboratories), they can be nominated by the community (as in Mars) or they can emerge as the natural leader based on their passion and energy. They can be called coordinators or facilitators or leaders or minders – whatever terminology is acceptable to the community. In a small community, the coordinator role may be part-time. In a larger community, say of more than 500 members, the coordinator role should be full-time. This is especially true if the community knowledge is of strategic value.

A core team

Sometimes a community facilitator may need a core team to help them run the community. In Mars, this is represented by a steering team of senior, experienced associates who set the agenda for the coming year and control the centrally focused activities. In other communities, the core team is a set of self-appointed practitioners who voluntarily take a hand in managing the community business.

Critical mass

Communities of practice need a certain amount of interaction in order to remain in the consciousness of the community members and therefore to be a source of learning that people naturally turn to. They can suffer from 'out of sight, out of mind', and a community that is too small or too preoccupied to be sufficiently active will begin to lose its sense of identity and people will forget it is there. The community coordinator therefore needs to build membership and grow the community as fast as possible after launch to keep the momentum going and to get to critical mass. This will require a combination of internal marketing, advertising, awareness-raising and direct invitation to people who might be interested. This is likely to take a considerable portion of the community coordinator's time in the first few months after launch. Each potential new member needs to be welcomed into the community, introduced to the terms of reference and encouraged to take part in knowledge-sharing, thus building mass one member at a time. The size of the critical mass varies depending on the intensity of the learning, the passion of the individuals and how diverse they are culturally and geographically. For a co-located community of passionate experts working in a new field, the critical mass may be a dozen people. For a global community working in an established field, exchanging knowledge through e-mail and online, the critical mass may be several hundred people. In Chapter 9, Mars describe how they moved from a model of many small communities to one of a few large communities in order to build critical mass more quickly.

A way to find each other

Communities must be visible. Staff must be able to find relevant communities, they must be able to join them easily and they must be able to see who else is a community member. There should ideally be, in the organisation, some index or 'yellow pages' for the communities.

A community knowledge library

A community working on common processes and common topics needs their own knowledge library. This may be a community space within the corporate knowledge library discussed in Chapter 6, while many large communities will have their own portal. The InTouchSupport.com system in Schlumberger, for example, cost $160 million to develop a knowledge base to store and share knowledge on technical solutions for the technical service community. Because technology support is Schlumberger's main business, the company felt that this investment was worthwhile. By cutting 95 per cent from the time it takes to answer a technical question, it adds a claimed annual value of $200 million, through giving Schlumberger staff the ability to solve technical problems very rapidly in a business where time is money.

Smaller communities may develop their own knowledge library, perhaps on a SharePoint site or as a community wiki. A community blog is often very useful as well to notify the community of any new lessons, new knowledge or updated processes in the library.

A social network

Communities of practice are one particular type of social network – a social network with the purpose of collective learning. The members of a community are happy to share lessons and knowledge with each other because they feel a sense of identity with each other and they are even happier to share their lessons with community members whom they know personally and feel a social connection with. Much work has been done in the field of knowledge management on building social networks and on the concept of social network analysis. This involves mapping out the social links and the interactions within a community in order to assess the level of connectivity of the individuals. The community coordinator should be using any means possible to improve social connectivity, including the use of social software where appropriate. Social connectivity forms the groundwork for developing trust within the community, and trust is an essential ingredient if knowledge is to be shared and reused. However, assured and systematic learning within the community needs to transcend the social networks and the community needs to develop processes and approaches for accessing the knowledge of people they don't know and have never met. Approaches such as the discussion forums described above allow knowledge-sharing to take place within an entire community, regardless of how socially connected the individuals may be.

A level of autonomy

In allowing communities of practice to exist and operate, the organisation is accepting that much of the knowledge lies with the practitioners and that unwritten lessons can effectively be shared between the practitioners. The organisation must therefore give the practitioners enough autonomy to act on the lessons they receive. They should be empowered to reuse lessons, best practices and process improvements that have been validated by the community, without necessarily getting their line manager to revalidate them every time. This does not mean that all decision-making is delegated to community members, but it means that line management can delegate a certain level of technical assurance to the communities. Disempowered communities rapidly become cynical and disaffected, which can become a bigger problem for management than having no communities at all.

External linkage

Marketing communities, in particular, may benefit from including external people, such as the marketing agencies, in order to be able to access their knowledge and experience. However, care must be taken when including more than one agency, particularly if they are in competition. They may not want to be as free and open with their knowledge if their competitors are listening in, or they may start to compete with each other, 'selling' their knowledge rather than sharing it objectively.

Communities of purpose

A community of purpose is a community of people from around the organisation, working within a single discipline. It differs from a community of practice in that these people are assigned to the community and the community of purpose is given (or sets itself) specific tasks and specific deliverables. The primary reason for a community of purpose is to develop organisational capacity and to deliver organisational results, in contrast with the community of practice where the purpose is to develop individual capacity and help individuals produce better results. Communities of purpose go under many names; Mars and Aon call them Global Practice Groups, BP calls them Delivery Networks, other organisations may call them expert communities or networks of excellence. The following is the Mars definition of Global Practice Groups (see Chapter 9):

> (Communities of purpose are) small groups of senior associates who are charged with delivering a step change in performance in an area of strategic importance to the company.

For a community of purpose to operate effectively as a mechanism for sharing knowledge, it needs the following enablers:

A business sponsor

The community of purpose needs an active sponsor at a high level within the organisation (in Mars, at the level of the Presidents Group), who has accountability for success of the particular discipline. For example, the head of sales would be the sponsor for any sales communities of purpose, the head of marketing would be the sponsor for any marketing communities of purpose, and so on. The sponsor is responsible for ensuring the community has what it needs to succeed, in terms of resource, space and time to operate, and empowerment. Through discussion with the core team, the sponsor will agree what the community goals should be and how they will be measured and will sign off on the community performance contract. The sponsor should also help set the leadership style, if communities are a new way of working, and should ensure that the results are visible across the business.

A leader and a delivery structure

The community of purpose needs a leader. Whereas a community of practice can operate with a facilitator, a community of purpose actually needs to define a leader who can take accountability for effective running of the community and for effective delivery of the community performance contract. The leader will be appointed by the sponsor and will almost certainly be a senior and respected player within the discipline, perhaps one of the company experts. The leader provides overall leadership and direction for the community, organises and runs community meetings and works together with the community sponsor to develop community objectives and to agree and draft the community performance contract.

The leader will also work with the core community members to develop plans to deliver these objectives and will coordinate and follow up the activities of the community to ensure that the community delivers its goals. He or she will maintain activity and energy within the community (Mars describe the leader as the 'Energiser Bunny' of the group in Chapter 9) and will set the working culture and open style of community working, ensuring that there is reward and recognition of the community members and that feedback is given on any value they have delivered.

A performance contract with well-defined deliverables

We have mentioned performance contracts a couple of times, and holding a performance contract differentiates a community of purpose from the community of practice. The performance contract is an agreement between the sponsor and the community that defines what the community aims to deliver in return for funding. This delivery is generally expressed in terms of business deliverables, such as 'achieve global sales growth of five per cent by building and sharing best practices in online marketing', plus a number of steps to achieve that deliverable. The performance contract should ideally be built 'bottom up' by the community itself, then agreed (or challenged) by the sponsor.

Funding

The community of purpose will need a budget. This will include a budget for community meetings and travel, a time-writing budget for the community leader and potentially the core community team. The community may also need money to commission some research activities or trials on behalf of the organisation. The scale of the budget will be agreed between the community leader and the sponsor, and the sponsor will generally provide the budget from his or her own funds.

Committed membership

The community of purpose needs a committed core team. This is likely to be made up from experts and practitioners selected from the different business units, countries and regions. The core team are usually assigned, rather than being volunteers, or at least are specifically invited to join the community. There may be additional roles within the core team; some organisations assign a deputy leader, some assign a manager or facilitator and many will assign a secretary to take notes and look after logistics.

A community collaboration space

The community of purpose will work together to deliver best practice to the organisation. They therefore need a site where they can collaborate, store information and share knowledge on a continuous basis. This site could include community contacts and resources, community news and publications (for example a community blog), work in progress in the form of documents or wikis, a community calendar and a community discussion forum.

Meetings

The community of purpose should hold face-to-face meetings at least once a year, as these physical meetings are vital for building and maintaining the relationships and trust within the team, which will be necessary for effective sharing of expertise and knowledge. Given that the team is dispersed, shorter follow-up meetings will be through telephone, video and web conferences, but the community should also aim to hold a face-to-face meeting in each major region of the world at least once a year.

A supporting community of practice

Very often a community of purpose will cover the same area of practice as a community of practice. In this case, the community of purpose can act as a core team for the practice community. The core team members are the ones responsible for delivering the performance contract, the ones who have been assigned to the community of purpose, the ones invited to the community meetings and the ones who can time-write (record their time on their timesheet against the community activities) to the community budget. The members of the community of practice have no responsibility for the performance contract, are volunteers and cannot time-write. They interact with the community through online discussion and may not have full access to the community collaboration space. A community of practice with a community of purpose at the core is an example of a nested community (Figure 4.2).

Communities of purpose are used in both marketing and sales and in Mars have had widespread use in sales (see for example the Route to Mass Market GPG described in Chapter 9).

Another case study of the use of communities of purpose within sales and marketing comes from Aon Insurance. Aon set up nine communities of purpose (which they call Global Practice Groups) to cover sales,

Figure 4.2   Nested communities

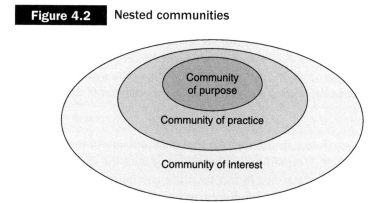

marketing and client support in their nine major global markets, such as Aviation and Aerospace, Marine and Property, each one under the lead of an executive sponsor. The purpose of the Global Practice Groups is to provide Aon's client managers and executives with the very latest knowledge and information to help solve clients' risk issues and so win business and sell insurance. According to the chairman of Aon's Property Global Practice Group, Nick Maher, 'we transact thousands of property deals every day across a broad range of businesses. Through our network of global contacts, we are able to tap into that database and compile industry-specific reports that quickly and credibly demonstrate Aon's depth of experience and global reach in every major industry sector. We have already seen that these reports have the power to differentiate Aon from our competitors.'[2]

Sarah Adams of Aon tells this success story:[3]

> Aon Australia's Melbourne office received an invitation to tender for the insurance business of a leading Australasian toll-road company, which was held by one of Aon's major competitors. The timeframe for the tender submission was very tight, allowing for little time to gather data and statistics. The Australian account director sent an e-mail to the Property GPG requesting urgent benchmarking information that would demonstrate Aon's global expertise in the field of toll roads, tunnels and bridges.
>
> Information on the insurance cover of similar companies was quickly collected from across the globe and compiled by Oliver Schofield, manager of the Property GPG. Property experts from China, Hong Kong, Canada, Brazil and Belgium sent details regarding their clients' cover, which were anonymised to protect their identities – a good data protection policy.
>
> The practice group was able to visibly demonstrate exactly what the toll company's international peers were paying for property cover and provide details about limits and deductibles. Within 24 hours, Aon's Melbourne office received the information; two days later the presentation was made to the company and less than two weeks after that Aon Melbourne was appointed as the new broker.

This case study demonstrates the role that a community of purpose can play in compiling information that bid teams around the world can use, in this case very successfully. In fact the story continues, as Aon Ireland shortly afterwards were bidding for an account for a toll-road in Ireland

and were able to use the knowledge and information from the Australian account to win the Irish account as well.

Communities of interest

A community of interest is a community of people interested in a particular topic. It is not necessarily their core practice area, but it's something they're interested in. They may work with this topic, they may be customers of this product, they may be people with a particular problem or medical condition who could potentially be consumers of a product – the link is that they all have an interest in this topic or item. Communities of interest can exist within your organisation or can extend beyond your organisation to cover your customer base, your suppliers or your partners. The flow of knowledge and information within a community of interest is usually outwards from the core team to the interested parties. There is also a lot of value in promoting a two-way flow, so that you can learn from your customer base or you can learn from people applying a product.

For a community of interest to work well, it needs the following enablers:

A core team to coordinate the communication

The community of interest thrives on communication and on information and needs a core communications team to make sure that the information flows and that the knowledge libraries are kept up to date. This team may be as small as one person or maybe a larger team with a team leader, depending on the scale of the community and the degree of information that needs to be broadcast. An external community of interest, catering to a large community of customers, will need a permanent core team to coordinate this.

A very good knowledge of the needs of the community members

Whether the community of interest is a group of people within your organisation working with a particular product or whether it is a customer community with an interest in a particular brand, you need to understand these people very well and understand what their information and knowledge needs are. You may need to do some internal and external market research before you can plan your community strategy.

Communication tools

The community of interest needs to be able to subscribe to communications, in order to be kept up to date on their area of interest. The communication tool could be a blog, an e-mail mailing list, a Twitter feed or a newsletter to notify the community of new products, changes to existing products and upcoming events. For example, Pepsi currently[4] have an @Pepsi Twitter feed with nearly 30,000 followers. They use this to interact with customers, announce events, promote products and encourage people to send in photographs of Pepsi products being consumed all over the world. Ben and Jerry's in France have a blog promoting products, activities and their French roadshow.[5] Dove has had great success releasing viral marketing videos on YouTube[6] in order to market Dove within the customer community, as has Old Spice. The Purina puppy club[7] is another example – a community of interest of puppy owners, sponsored by Purina pet foods. New puppy owners join the community and Purina sends them regular e-mail newsletters and updates as their puppy grows, thus providing them with information on the stages of puppy growth and at the same time subtly reinforcing the Purina brand.

Community discussion

A large part of the value from a customer community of interest comes from the ability to listen to the customer. The community of interest can conduct polls, seek feedback from customers or just listen to customer discussion. Many of the pharmaceutical communities of interest, for example, are focused on particular medical conditions and offer community interaction to allow sufferers to discuss the condition and its treatment and provide support for each other. At the same time, the pharmaceutical company can seek to understand the customer base better and so provide products that will help them. An example of this is Fibrocentre,[8] the fibromyalgia community site sponsored by Pfizer. As well as providing a whole set of educational resources about the condition, this site hosts a series of 'real patient stories' and invites community members to send in their own stories. The Herceptin site,[9] sponsored by

Roche, goes further and hosts a community of HER2+ breast cancer patients, allowing connections between women fighting breast cancer, for sharing of experiences and for mutual support. The Tesco baby club[10] provides a range of resources for new mothers, including a discussion forum where new mums can exchange hints on where to find maternity wear or how to encourage baby to sleep through the night. This club builds a sense of community among the young mums, promotes brand awareness and allows Tesco to promote new products such as baby food, clothes and nappies (diapers).

Knowledge base

The community of interest needs a knowledge base where they can find the core knowledge about their particular topic of interest. For an internal community, this will be a SharePoint site or a portal where they can find information on a particular product or a particular brand. The customer communities of interest that we have discussed above also contain knowledge bases. The Tesco baby and toddler club, for example, contains a wealth of advice for new parents, guiding them through their children's development and including items such as an A to Z of child health, recipes for healthy eating, exercise and makeover tips and of course a whole range of in-store special offers. The fibromyalgia site has a whole series of guidelines on living with fibromyalgia, including a compilation of tips from other sufferers. The Amex 'open forum' for business owners[11] provides links to experts, links to guidance for small businesses, as well as a discussion forum and a Twitter feed. They also provide a service rather like an online knowledge market (see Chapter 3), where small businesses can link with others who might be able to help them.

A social network

Part of the purpose of building a community of interest, either inside the company or with customers, is to build a social network. This is particularly important with customers, as this will underpin brand loyalty going forwards. Social networking tools can be particularly important here and many organisations are using these tools to build their customer communities of interest. However, it is important that marketers who intend to use these tools participate in a way that is sensitive and will be welcomed by the users. Users are highly empowered and not shy of stating their opinion, and a company that gets this wrong will get it publicly wrong.

An example of an organisation using social networking tools to build a powerful community of interest is the use of Facebook by Guinness. Guinness UK have a very attractive Facebook site[12] with nearly 300,000 supporters, containing customer photographs, links to promotional articles, customer comments, a calendar of upcoming events and the Guinness Pubfinder.

Similarly, the Toyota Prius has its own Facebook site, with 55,000 supporters. On their site they even provide an 'ask an expert' service, a set of videos and a neat little game called 'acts of kindness', where people collaborate to suggest eco-friendly tips.

For brands with a very positive customer perception, this type of Facebook activity can really strengthen brand loyalty. Without existing brand loyalty, it can have less of an effect. This book was written at the time of the BP oil spill, and while BP America's Facebook page[13] had 33,000 supporters, this was heavily outnumbered by the Boycott BP page,[14] with 775,000 supporters.

Notes

1. Otherwise known as the community facilitator, community moderator, community leader or community minder.
2. 'Practice makes perfect', Sarah Adams, *Inside Knowledge* magazine, volume 9, issue 4, December 2004.
3. Ibid.
4. Summer 2010.
5. *http://www.benjerry.fr/blog/*
6. *http://www.youtube.com/watch?v=iYhCn0jf46U*
7. *http://www.purina.com.au/puppy-kitten-club/puppy-kitten-club.aspx*
8. *http://www.fibrocenter.com/index.aspx*
9. *http://www.herceptin.com/index.jsp*
10. *http://www.tesco.com/babyclub/*
11. *http://www.openforum.com/*
12. *http://www.facebook.com/Guinnessgb*
13. *http://www.facebook.com/BPAmerica*
14. *http://www.facebook.com/BoycottBP*

5

Technology

In this chapter we will review technology and how it can be used to support knowledge management in the sales, bidding and marketing areas. We will look at 'traditional' technology, such as the CRM databases and also at the emerging web 2.0 technology that supports social networks and communities of practice. There is no shortage of technology in these fields and what seems to be more important in delivering effective knowledge management is that the technology is appropriate to the style of the company. For example, BT is participating in a state-of-the-art experiment, described in Chapter 8, to develop technology that will provide their sales staff and technical consultants with easier access to knowledge and with improved and streamlined processes. They are a technology company and their people are comfortable with technology. Finding that they are pushing the boundaries of technology to help their people work with customers is therefore no surprise. It fits naturally with the style of the organisation. The approach that Mars take to the use of technology, described in Chapter 9, also matches the style of the organisation. Mars are very much a 'people company' and while they use technology as an enabler, it is mostly the more traditional technology of case stories, websites and training courses, albeit with an increasing number of wikis.

It is very tempting to think that all you need to do is purchase the latest software, CRM system, wiki, blog or smartphone and your knowledge management performance will dramatically improve. That is not necessarily true. As Graeme Smith says in Chapter 10:

> *Enterprise-wide knowledge management systems are not a panacea for solving the problems of sharing knowledge in a company that aspires to be a learning organisation. Important though such systems are, it is the successful management of business processes as well as the cultural issues that relate to the way people are prepared and have an ability to share knowledge that is of fundamental importance.*

However, the combination of the right technology, the right learning processes, the right roles and the right governance will create an effective and powerful knowledge management framework. Let us now look at some of the technologies that can form part of the framework, starting with the most basic.

The telephone

The telephone is perhaps the most overlooked piece of technology in today's business environment. The basic voice telephone, whether sitting on a desk or a mobile device, allows people to instantly request advice and guidance or share what they know with others. Telephone conference calls at which attendees can participate from almost anywhere are an ideal way for a dispersed team to stay in touch. They can listen as knowledge is revealed to them or they can provide an update on the current status of their work. The telephone is the technology foundation for knowledge management as it connects people to people. As Linda Davies says in Chapter 9, 'The key is to match what we are trying to achieve with the natural style of the associates concerned . . . how they naturally work and therefore how they will access the knowledge and use it. . . . As a sweeping generalisation (and accepting there are notable exceptions!) the preferred communication style of our sales people is the telephone (assuming they cannot get face to face).'

Increasingly, however, the telephone is morphing into something altogether smarter. Android phones, iPhones and BlackBerries all offer the possibility to link the mobile workforce with collaboration tools and online to company-hosted databases. Increasingly, the telephone becomes another interface to access community tools and knowledge bases.

Community software

Community software is the equipment that allows you to interact with your community by asking questions, starting discussions, alerting people to things and finding people. Traditionally, this was done using discussion forums and membership lists, but nowadays the range of options is much greater.

Discussion forums and Q&A forums are places on the Internet or an intranet where users can post messages for others to read, answer and comment on. Often the discussion is hosted on a website, while users interact through their e-mail system. Various e-mails or posts are presented as 'threads', with each thread being a single topic and with the posts presented in chronological order. There are many options for in-house discussion forums within a community, including SharePoint, Lotus Notes, Outlook public folders and bespoke applications. Discussion forums are for open discussion within a community, with discussions often lasting for a long time and frequently changing focus over time (known as 'topic drift'). Q&A forums are one type of discussion forum, specifically for asking and answering questions. An employee can raise a question on a specific topic and anyone in the community with knowledge or advice to share can answer. Some Q&A forums send the questions only to a group of experts (such as the 'Ask Anglo' system in AngloAmerican). Others send them to the whole community. Q&A forums are 'ask the audience' technology, in the language of *Who Wants to be a Millionaire?* They can be a lifeline for individuals isolated from their community of practice. Any company looking to build strong internal communities of practice should invest in discussion and Q&A functionality.

Social networking sites such as Facebook and LinkedIn also have discussion capability for interaction between community members. If your plan is to build an external community of interest involving your customer base, then you may need to use one of the commercially available social networking sites. Increasingly there are options for building social networking within your organisation to support your communities of practice. SalesForce Chatter, for example, will allow your marketing staff to interact with each other from their desks in a Facebook style and will do the same for your salesforce using their mobile devices. Chatter even includes links to Twitter, allowing staff to use the restricted 140-character alerts, which then can be expanded into proper collaborative discussions. As described in the previous chapter, Twitter can also be used to support an external community of interest.

Blogs are increasingly being used as a mechanism to disseminate information to a community of practice or a community of interest. Within an internal marketing community, for example, the community core team could maintain a blog to showcase new material, to inform people of changes to marketing best practice and to announce internal events and conferences. Externally, blogs are increasingly being used as a type of 'infomercial' and a way to cross-link to selling sites. See for example the Avis blog, 'We try harder',[1] showcasing various aspects of Avis service, the Nokia Conversations blog[2] promoting new applications, or the Nike Basketball blog[3] with its cross-linking to Nike products and brands.

A **yellow pages** system is an index of 'who knows what' – a knowledge directory for the internal community of practice or for the organisation. It enables you to find people to help you and to help people find you. It is an easy way to locate anyone working in the business, based on their knowledge and expertise. The system allows you to create your own personal home page, including your contact details, your picture, your CV and links to other information – in fact, anything you want to say about yourself. Yellow pages can link with information already held about you on other databases, such as the company e-mail directory. Yellow pages can also create membership lists for communities and allow you to search for communities as well as individuals. Social networking software often gives people the capability to create their own personal pages, but seldom allows a taxonomy-based search.

A video conference is a meeting of people to 'confer' about a topic, where the people are in more than one location, but can use two-way video and audio transmissions to hear and see each other. Traditionally video conferences have used large expensive boardroom-style rooms, but increasingly people are using desktop videoconferencing in the style of Skype or Live Messenger to interact with their colleagues in other parts of the organisation. Effective videoconferencing is greatly helped if the attendees have already met face to face and so know each other. It is less useful as a format for meeting people for the first time.

Collaboration software

This is software used by a community of purpose or a group of people working together to complete a document or a knowledge product. There are many types of collaboration software, with Microsoft SharePoint and Lotus Notes probably leading the field, but many other software companies are entering this area, for example Opentext (which allows collaboration on the move through mobile devices). Increasingly, collaboration within communities of practice and communities of purpose is done through wikis. A wiki is a website that allows staff to edit, including adding and deleting, content. These collaborative tools initially found favour among groups who were jointly creating complex documents such as standards and manuals. However, as the technology evolved and the ease of use of the wiki sites increased, they began to be used to retain and build best practice in a form that allows them to be annotated by others.

Wikis in a sales and marketing context are often used to support internal communities of practice. A sales community can collaborate to build sales FAQs and product descriptions or a marketing community can collaborate to build their corporate marketing best practices. Kris Duggan, Head of Sales at Socialtext, describes[4] using a sales wiki to track activity at account level:

> *Here at Socialtext, we use SugarCRM and also publish comments and activities for our accounts into our sales wiki using 'wiki web services'. Watching the 'What's New' page, you can quickly see what is happening across the entire team at the account level. A quick read at the end of the day or prior to a strategy session provides immediate context on our pipeline growth, opportunities for coaching and overall level of activity across the team. I've never seen this level of openness available in a stand-alone CRM tool and I think the combined solution is quite unique and powerful.*

Chapter 8 describes a research programme at BT in the use of a semantic wiki[5] to support a bidding community in their preparation of proposals for clients. Here the bid community is expected to use the wiki to store not only the technical information needed to answer client questions when writing a proposal, but also to link and to be able to search for the experts who can 'fill in the gaps' if new questions are asked.

Knowledge libraries

The knowledge library represents a structured repository for guidance, good practice, knowledge assets and useful documents and examples. A marketing community might maintain a knowledge library of marketing campaign material that others can copy and adapt or a library of market research reports. A bid community might maintain a knowledge library of bid 'boilerplate text', which can be reused in future bids. There are a number of possibilities for technology to support a knowledge library. The simplest is a shared file structure: either a set of folders on the drive or a set of files within a SharePoint site. More complex than this, but far easier to browse and use, is a portal. The third option is a wiki (described above).

Knowledge portals

Most companies have a web-based system or portal for structuring and storing internal knowledge, so that it can be accessed through a web browser. Corporate intranets became more popular as organisations started to realise that they could provide a simple route, via a web browser, to a library of company information and explicit knowledge. As the demand for the provision of portals grew, so too did the tools that the IT department could use to create and manage content. Today it's not unusual for company employees to be able to publish directly to the company portal and portals are becoming more and more customised to the needs of the individual user. Portals have also been seen as away of integrating legacy applications in organisations, a situation that frequently occurs when one organisation is acquired by another.

One problem with portals is that it can often be very difficult to add content. For well-established and mature processes, this is not a problem, as content will only rarely be added or updated. However, for process knowledge that is dynamically evolving, it can be extremely useful to allow the readers to comment on the documentation or even to edit it, as new lessons are learned and new knowledge becomes available. This is where wikis can add huge value.

Search

Any knowledge library needs a good search engine. There are many options for enterprise search and there are few organisations now without good search functionality.

RSS feeds

Really simple syndication (RSS) is a way for people to subscribe to relevant blogs, databases, portals and websites in order to be notified of any new content. New lessons and new process improvements can be automatically forwarded to your RSS reader as soon as they are published, without needing to browse the websites. Each individual may need to download an RSS reader to their own computer and then visit the websites and blogs they wish to subscribe to. However, many organisations provide these as a standard tool and anyone who uses Microsoft Outlook 2007 will find that it can be used as a perfectly acceptable RSS reader.

Tagging

Tagging provides an alternative option to the built-in taxonomy or ontology for indexing a lessons database. Both the benefit and weakness of a taxonomy are its rigidity. By allowing content providers to tag lessons with the most likely terms and then allowing the customers to also apply their own tags, tagging can provide a more dynamic means of giving access to lessons in a way that truly relates to the needs of the users, provided of course that the system allows for tag-based queries. Chapter 8 describes an investigation that BT are carrying out into user tagging of information, as part of the ACTIVE research project, in order to provide rapid access to relevant information by their home-based sales staff.

Tagging and the user-created taxonomies, known as 'folksonomies', have their drawbacks in that tags are user-created and are often more relevant to the supplier of the knowledge than to the seeker of the knowledge.[6] BT plan to overcome this drawback by combining tagging with a lightweight ontology, allowing users two approaches to classifying information and therefore providing more than one way for others to find it (see Chapter 8 for details).

Customer databases and product databases

Customer relationship management (CRM) systems are in effect specialised lessons learned systems. Instead of containing a wide variety of lessons on a variety of topics, they are focused on storing lessons and background material on customers. In many instances, however, CRM is treated as an IT project instead of a tool to be used on a day-to-day basis by sales staff. There are a huge number of CRM products on the market, easily more than 800 and counting, so it is vital that the people who are going to use them are involved in the purchasing decision. CRM also needs to be supported by business processes that are effective, otherwise it is like putting a Ferrari engine in a ten-year-old car – the engine is great but the gearbox and suspension aren't compatible with it and something is going to break. The other matter to be aware of when selecting the CRM system is what could be described as 'enhanced features'. Does your organisation really need all the functionality that is on offer by the vendor?

The benefits that CRM will bring to the individual employee need to be explained in advance. If you can't sell the CRM system to your staff, it is very unlikely that they will use it. What are the things that they currently find challenging? How will the CRM system assist them to overcome that? Sales people want to spend time with customers, so look for vendor support such as webinars that illustrate to your staff how to use the CRM system to increase their closing rate.

Tools such as Landslide (www.landslide.com) allows the sales manager not only to see what is in the sales pipeline but also what activities are occurring (or not occurring) in every opportunity within the pipeline. It also allows the manager to monitor what steps have been completed in the sales process. But perhaps the most interesting aspect of tools such as these is the way in which they start to capture the buyers' interests and behaviours. Tools such as these link process-based selling software with document retrieval so that the sales person no longer has to search for documents and presentations; they are linked to the stage of the sale cycle they are in.

Product databases are frequently used by call centre operatives to respond to requests from customers. First contract resolution (FCR) is an important metric used by call centres to measure how effective they are in handling customers' contacts and resolving issues. Frequently a product database is the backbone of these systems and provides 'product knowledge' to the sales person handling the call. Systems such as SalesForce (www.salesforce.com) allow the collective experience of selling and handling calls to be combined so that everyone can learn from each other; knowledge is shared.

An approach that is becoming increasingly common is the 'self-help' approach. The product database is made available to customers and they are encouraged to search and find their own answers. Each time 'a solution' is presented the customer is asked to rank how useful it was; the more useful, the more that solution is presented in future. This self-help system has the advantage that it has reduced the amount of time agents spend on routine questions, sparing them for the more unusual or difficult issues. Systems such as Kayako (www.kayako.com) also monitor trends and, as they record knowledge as it is created or used, there is less potential for knowledge leak from the organisation. From the agent's perspective, one of the most significant developments has been in the development of the automated answers system. Kayako, SalesForce and ServiceDeskPlus will proactively suggest to the agent solutions to the issue as the agent types in the description of the problem. This saves time and greatly assists in situations where staff turnover is high or multiple locations are used to service one product. These are all examples of product databases proactively supporting the sales and marketing staff.

The terminology 'CRM and knowledge management' has become blurred in some instances. Knowledge management not only contains technology such as collaboration software but it also includes people (roles and responsibilities) and processes (activities).

Notes

1. *http://www.wetryharder.co.uk/*
2. *http://conversations.nokia.com/*
3. *http://inside.nike.com/blogs/nikebasketball*
4. *http://www.socialtext.com/blog/2006/10/113/*
5. A semantic wiki is one in which, in creating a link between two pages, authors may associate semantics with the link.
6. A significant number of people in Flickr use the tag 'Me' when describing a picture – a tag that is useful only to the person who took the picture.

6

Knowledge management roles

As we said in Chapter 2, knowledge roles need to be created in a business to make sure that knowledge management is embedded in the business activity. Without knowledge roles, knowledge management becomes 'everyone's job' and very quickly reverts to being nobody's job. The key knowledge management roles within this environment are the knowledge manager, the knowledge management champion, the knowledge librarian, the community facilitator, the subject matter expert (SME), the central knowledge management team and the senior sponsor.

The knowledge managers and the knowledge management champions form part of the line management structure, shown in Regions 1 and 2 of Figure 6.1. This is the structure of regions and countries or assets and business units and teams who are primarily responsible for delivery of sales and marketing targets. The community leaders and the knowledge owners may sit within this structure or they may be part of the central support groups, reporting to the head of sales, head of marketing or head of bidding. The knowledge management team will most likely be a separate team reporting directly to senior management. More detail on these roles follows.

Knowledge manager

The knowledge manager is the person who 'makes KM happen' at the level of a team or a business group. Much as a project leader may set up a safety role within a project to make sure the project complies with safety expectations or set up a quality role within a manufacturing unit to make sure the unit complies with quality expectations, so they may set up a knowledge management role to make sure KM happens. This

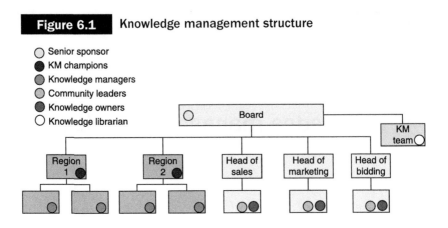

Figure 6.1   Knowledge management structure

role might be described as the **knowledge manager** for that team, business unit or project.

The knowledge manager makes sure that the team or project that they are working with are doing the knowledge management that they are supposed to do. They make sure that the expected knowledge management processes happen at the right time and that the expected knowledge management technologies are applied at the right time. They ensure that staff get the knowledge they need, that this knowledge gets applied to the work and that new knowledge is captured and shared. They work by mentoring, coaching, facilitating and prompting to make sure that KM processes happen and that KM technologies are used. They are the people who translate 'KM processes and tools' into actions and activities that the sales and marketing professionals can understand and implement. The ideal knowledge manager is a people-centred personality who derives great reward from seeing others succeed. They tend to work in the background – educating, helping and assisting others to achieve their goals.

This role might be particularly important, for example, in a busy bid team, to make sure that enough attention is paid to knowledge management despite the hectic activity of bidding.

Knowledge management champion

The knowledge management champion is somebody at a relatively high level in a business unit or region, who acts to promote knowledge management within that part of the business. Their role is not as practical a role as that of a knowledge manager; it's more of an evangelical or promotional role. The knowledge management champion works with senior managers to ensure that knowledge management is promoted at all levels and co-operates with the knowledge managers to ensure that it actually gets done in practice. Sometimes the knowledge management champion and the knowledge manager are the same person, but more often the champion takes the lead for a region, within which there may be many knowledge managers.

Knowledge librarian

The knowledge librarian looks after the knowledge library or the company knowledge base. They do not create and update the content within the library, but they make sure that the knowledge library is well maintained, well structured and easy to use. The knowledge librarian may have several roles:

- They may act as champions for the knowledge library, ensuring that people are aware of it and of the value it can deliver.
- They may provide training and support in the use of the knowledge library.
- They may work with IT to ensure the technology behind the knowledge library is appropriate, with all the functionality required by the users.
- They may work with the business to ensure that the knowledge library has an effective taxonomy and any required tags or metadata.
- They may work with the knowledge owners to ensure that they are fulfilling their responsibilities and making sure that content is relevant, usable, up to date and stored in the correct place.
- They may monitor the use of the knowledge library and report statistics, such as the number of readers, the number of authors, the frequency of update, etc.

Community facilitator or leader

The role of the community facilitator or community leader has been covered in detail in Chapter 4.

Subject matter experts (SMEs) and knowledge owners

In knowledge management terms, the central sales and marketing teams have two main functions:

- First, they are responsible for managing subject matter knowledge on behalf of the organisation. So the head of marketing and his team are accountable for managing the company's knowledge about marketing; and for making sure that this knowledge is up to date, accessible and available for the marketers within the business. Similarly, the head of sales and her function are accountable for managing the company's sales knowledge, making sure that the company 'knows how to sell' – that they have the knowledge they need, when they need it, in order to operate to the required standard. They will do this through appointing **knowledge owners** (also known as subject matter experts or knowledge stewards).

- Second, they are accountable for ensuring that there are **communities of practice** through which this knowledge can be shared. Very often, the head of sales, the head of marketing and the head of bidding act as sponsors for the sales community, the marketing community and the bidding community.

Knowledge owners are individuals who have the role of managing or stewarding company knowledge in one specific topic area. They are experts on their topic. So the head of marketing may, for example, appoint a knowledge owner for online marketing, a knowledge owner for TV campaigns and a knowledge owner for print ads.

The accountability that goes with this role is to keep the knowledge base up to date in this topic, so that people in the business who need this knowledge can find it easily and know that it is valid, up to date and presented in a usable format. They may be responsible for ensuring that the knowledge library is populated with content covering this topic. They may provide internal consultancy on the topic, although their role is not to keep hold of the knowledge themselves; their role is to share it and to make it widely available. They monitor the state of knowledge of the topic; they build and maintain the knowledge base, constructing the wikis or reference sites and keeping them up to date. They validate and broadcast new knowledge and make sure training in the topic is available and up to date. They are the 'go to' people for their topic.

Sometimes people play this role by default and Chapter 10 (the case study from the Ordnance Survey) describes people spending 80 per cent of their time as the de facto subject matter expert and only 20 per cent of their time doing the work in their job description. It is obviously better to make it their real job!

The central knowledge management team

During the implementation stage, a knowledge management project is set up to implement change in the organisation and to move the organisation to a state where knowledge management is embedded as part of the business. Like any project, there are a number of roles and accountabilities associated with delivering the project objectives. These include the KM project leader. The role of the KM project leader is an absolutely crucial one. This person delivers the KM implementation, leads the implementation team and manages the budget. Their accountability is clear. They are responsible for delivering the project objectives, within the agreed time frame and to the agreed cost and standard. Choosing the right person for this role is also very important. The KM project leader needs to be a respected member of the organisation, with a history of delivering organisational change.

In anything other than a very small company, the KM project leader will need a KM implementation team. The size of the team and the specific roles within the team will vary from company to company. You may need somebody on the team with a communication role, responsible for making sure that knowledge management communications to the wider organisation are timely and relevant. You may need somebody on the team accountable for coordinating a KM community of practice. You may need somebody on the team accountable for ensuring that the technology suite is complete. If you are looking to implement through the use of pilot projects, there will also be clear accountabilities related to pilot project delivery. It all depends very much on what you need to do to get knowledge management up and running. Make sure that your KM team members have a good grounding in sales, marketing and bidding, so that they can easily translate knowledge management concepts into the language of business.

You sometimes hear people suggest that the KM implementation team should look to 'do themselves out of a job' and that the final aim of KM implementation should be that KM is fully embedded in the business. An end to implementation, with KM fully embedded, is a laudable aim – but this should not be taken as implying that there will be no requirement for a long-term KM support resource. Even after implementation is over and the KM system is designed and rolled out, you need a person or a small group to keep up the momentum.

Their main tasks will be to maintain the KM system (updating technology, training people in the processes, coaching individuals with KM roles), running the monitoring and measurement activities, crafting the longer-term KM strategy and making the necessary interventions to sustain KM. Part of the successful longevity of KM within BP Drilling is due to the presence of a KM support team over the past nine years.

Senior sponsor

The senior sponsor is the senior person, perhaps a board member, who will 'speak up' for knowledge management in senior meetings. They are the person who will ensure that knowledge management has adequate budget and resources and that it is seen as being a value-added activity for the organisation. The senior sponsor need not be an expert in KM but should have a commitment and passion for it. They also ensure that the KM work is fully aligned with current and future initiatives.

It is very important that the senior sponsor understands the environment that knowledge management will face within sales and marketing so that the knowledge management team will put in place something that is fit for purpose and will deliver the required knowledge management culture change.

7

Culture and governance

The issue of culture in knowledge management is key. Introducing knowledge management involves more than introducing the processes, technologies and roles mentioned in the previous chapters. It also involves introducing a new culture and introducing the governance system that sustains that culture. The culture change involved with introducing knowledge management is a profound shift from the individual to the collective ownership of knowledge:

- from 'I know' to 'we know';
- from 'knowledge is mine' to 'knowledge is ours';
- from 'knowledge is owned' to 'knowledge is shared';
- from 'knowledge is personal property' to 'knowledge is collective/ community property';
- from 'knowledge is personal advantage' to 'knowledge is company advantage';
- from 'knowledge is personal' to 'knowledge is interpersonal';
- from 'I defend what I know' to 'I am open to better knowledge';
- from 'not invented here (i.e. by me)' to 'invented in my community';
- from 'new knowledge competes with my personal knowledge' to 'new knowledge improves my personal knowledge';
- from 'other people's knowledge is a threat to me' to 'our shared knowledge helps me';
- from 'admitting I don't know is weakness' to 'admitting I don't know is the first step to learning'.

That shift from 'I know' to 'we know' and from 'knowledge is mine' to 'knowledge is ours' is a huge one and counter-cultural to many. People often attribute their success in an organisation and the salary and position that come from the success as due to their personal knowledge. To be asked to share their personal knowledge feels like being asked to relinquish power, rewards and security. People ask, 'What's in it for me?'

Chapter 10, the case study from the Ordnance Survey, describes some of the cultural barriers that mitigate against the flow of knowledge, including management and leadership, a lack of trust due to 'a blame culture' and the lack of defined boundaries between roles and responsibilities. We explore some of these barriers and influences below.

Knowledge management, target-setting and incentives

The conflict between personal rewards and security on the one hand and the organisational benefits of knowledge-sharing on the other is most obvious when it comes to target-setting and incentives. This is particularly clear in sales, where traditionally sales reps are given individual targets with a strong element of performance-related incentives. If they meet and exceed their targets, they can be highly rewarded, as well as recognised in various 'sales rep of the year' awards. Taking time out to share their tips and hints and knowledge with others not only distracts them from meeting their targets, but also potentially gives away some competitive benefit to people competing for those same targets.

In a sales team, it pays to think very carefully about target-setting. One sales manager we spoke to takes a counterintuitive approach to this in a bid to improve team knowledge-sharing. She assigns a team target for her team, for which the whole team is accountable. Then she assigns individual targets, set within the context of the team target, that are equal for every rep, regardless of their experience. So the most experienced sales representative gets the same target as the least experienced. This, she feels, is the fairest way to assign targets and avoid putting the whole burden on the experienced people while letting the juniors off lightly. Once the experienced staff have delivered their targets, they go on to help their less experienced colleagues, transferring knowledge in the process and helping to build a team spirit. All of the public praise and all of the public recognition is for the team target and none for the individual target. For this manager, there is no 'sales rep of the year'.

The role of the manager in setting the culture

We can see in the example above the key role that the manager plays in setting the sharing culture within the team. The manager needs to reinforce this sharing culture by setting expectations and by managing the conversations.

Where there are recognition and accolades for individual performance, as soon as that happens, the manager has to move the conversation on to how the team can duplicate and apply these successes elsewhere. 'There is never any bitterness about celebrating someone else's success,' one manager told us. 'The team just want to know "Great, how did you do it and how can we copy it?" And if a person does succeed, they are the first to say "and here is how you can apply it in your area".'

The manager has to promote the behaviour of sharing success and best practice to help one another. There may be natural reluctance to sharing success and best practice; people don't want to come across as boasting or maybe they don't recognise the value of what they know, and the manager has to be careful to foster and encourage the correct behaviours. Sharing success has to be voluntary, but the manager can coach individuals to share openly and can set time in team meetings for sharing success.

The manager has to promote the behaviour of sharing the challenges as well. If one of the sales team has been having trouble meeting their targets, which will be apparent when the sales figures are shared, the manager should always ask for the team input and ask the team to share their knowledge of what they think the situation might need.

The quote below shows how this sort of manager attention can change team culture:

> We have people who like to win and that is the key. When I first took on the team, they used to compete against one another. Now they compete only to increase the total results. How did I turn around the culture? I steered them in terms of the team results. I brought it up in the appraisals and also during all the other usual conversations in the team.

Dealing with inter-team competition

Of course this approach to team target-setting only develops a culture of knowledge-sharing within the team. Sales staff are naturally competitive people; they like to be winners and they like to compete. The first step is to build team collaboration, so that instead of having winners and losers within the team, the whole team become winners. However, they will still at this point want someone else to compete against. One sales manager said to us, 'We build a sense of team success. We talk about the team target and then the first thing they want to know is whether we are leading the way in Canada (i.e. beating the other teams).' So competition has been displaced from the team and replaced with inter-team competition.

However, for knowledge management to deliver its full potential, we need to look at knowledge-sharing not just within teams, but also between teams. How can we do this, when the teams perceive themselves to be rivals?

We do this by introducing structures that cross-cut the team structure. The communities of practice, communities of purpose and communities of interest all allow people to join something with membership from many teams. A sales representative in France could join a community of purpose on 'selling to major supermarket chains' and find herself at a workshop or knowledge exchange, working together with her counterparts in Australia and Mexico. Suddenly these people are not rivals, but allies. Communities are one of the most effective ways of introducing cross-team and cross-region sharing.

When it comes to identifying and sharing best practices, the central knowledge management team can play a role. Although a highly successful sales manager may not want to directly divulge his or her secrets to a rival sales manager, they might be perfectly happy to conduct an interview with the knowledge management team, even knowing that what they share with the knowledge management team will also be shared with the other sales departments. The difference of course is that this is two-way sharing; they will share, but they will receive in return. We have had great success gathering knowledge from sales managers and sales teams in this way.

Dealing with 'not invented here'

The matter of competition between team members and between teams is much less of an issue for bids teams and marketing teams than it is for sales. For marketing and bidding, the biggest barrier tends to be 'not invented here', rather than internal competition.

'Not invented here' is one of the most difficult barriers to overcome in knowledge management. It is seen in teams who prefer to create their own solutions, rather than reusing the knowledge and the solutions of others. It is a common barrier in very creative teams or in teams where they are using their collective experience to create a product. In these cases, people feel far more secure or far more creatively satisfied if they create the product purely from their own experience. Even if another team has done something very similar, they still feel more secure in starting from a blank sheet of paper. Basically, 'not invented here' is often a symptom of an unwillingness to learn and there is absolutely no point in creating the best knowledge-sharing system if your organisation has a learning problem.

There are various ways of discouraging 'not invented here' or subtly encouraging the reuse of knowledge, but if you are looking for a lasting and sustained culture change, ultimately 'not invented here' has to become unacceptable behaviour.

One way to address this is to refuse to approve any marketing campaign or bid document that has been 'only invented here'. The regional marketing director could make it clear that he or she will not approve a campaign that doesn't build on knowledge and material from successful campaigns elsewhere in the world. The bid director could stress that he or she will not sign off a bid document if there has been no peer assist with other bid teams to build on their knowledge and experience. At the same time, of course, you have to build the communities of practice and the knowledge libraries that make it easy to find what others have done and to reuse it.

Another leader refused to accept 'only invented here' by introducing what he calls 'no single-source solutions'. It is a stated point of principle within his part of the organisation to have no single-source solutions – solutions that have been worked up by one person with no input from other parts of the business. Single-source solutions represent 'only invented here' and by refusing to accept these, he gives the message that solutions have to be based on multiple inputs and external knowledge.

Knowledge management expectations

In the previous section, we saw examples of regional marketing managers or bid directors making their expectations for knowledge management very clear. Clear expectations are vital if the knowledge management culture is to be introduced, and everybody in sales, bidding and marketing needs to know what is expected of them in knowledge management terms. This expectation has to come down from senior management. They need to write these expectations down and keep reinforcing them by what they say and do. They also need to make sure these expectations do not get weakened by or conflict with other company structures and expectations, such as the incentive scheme (see above about setting team targets rather than individual targets).

One clear way to define expectations is to define an **in-house standard** for knowledge management. What does this mean in practice? What is an acceptable level of knowledge management activity? Does every bid project need to hold a retrospect, or only the big ones? Are peer assists a mandatory requirement for marketing campaigns, or optional? Does every sales representative need to update the CRM database after every sales call? You need to sit down with senior management and decide what the corporate KM standard is going to be.

Along with clarity on standards comes clarity on **accountability**. By accountability we mean, whose job is it to ensure learning and sharing? Whose responsibility is it to make sure that the knowledge base is updated? Who are the knowledge owners? Senior management will need to set up one or more chains of accountability, so that everyone in the organisation knows what is expected of them. We say 'one or more' chains – in many organisations there will be three chains of accountability, as shown in Figure 7.1.

There will certainly be a chain of accountability in the line organisation (Region 1 and Region 2 in Figure 7.1) – the organisation of business units that 'do the work'. Here the accountability will be about capturing new knowledge and reusing existing knowledge. For example, the head

Figure 7.1 Chains of KM accountability in an organisation

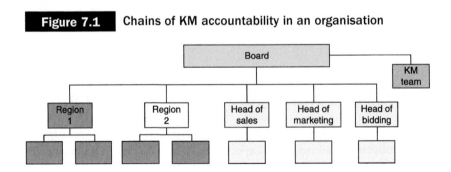

of European marketing may be accountable for ensuring that the European marketing division captures and shares its knowledge and uses knowledge from elsewhere in the world. He or she will devolve this accountability down to the country managers, who will in turn pass this down to the marketing teams.

In a matrix organisation, there may also be a chain of accountability in the functional or support departments. Here the accountability is likely to cover the ownership, maintenance and deployment of the company knowledge base and will include accountabilities for knowledge ownership and community leadership. The head of sales, for example, will be accountable for making sure that the company's sales processes are managed and updated and will ensure that the individual knowledge owners and community leaders are doing their jobs properly.

Finally, there will be a set of accountabilities for the knowledge management support team. These will include accountability for maintaining the knowledge management system and for monitoring and measuring its use.

Reinforcement

Knowledge management needs to be reinforced. People who perform well in knowledge management need to be recognised and those who do not conform to their accountabilities or to the corporate expectations may need to experience some sort of sanction.

Bob Buckman, the CEO of Buckman Laboratories, was very good at this. The KM team measured the use of the knowledge management tools by the sales and support staff at Buckman Laboratories and reported this to the CEO on a regular basis. Staff who were particularly good at sharing and reusing knowledge were rewarded with new laptops and with other non-monetary rewards. Staff who were not using the system would receive an e-mail that might say, 'Dear Associate, You have not been sharing knowledge. How may I help you?' And those associates who still refused to comply with the knowledge management expectations might receive an e-mail that says, 'If you are not willing to contribute or participate, then you should understand that the many opportunities open to you in the past will no longer be available.'[1]

Organisations that are serious about knowledge management have to take an approach similar to Bob Buckman's. He reinforced positive behaviours and sanctioned negative behaviours. People found that their personal involvement in knowledge management impacted their prospects and as a result Buckman Laboratories had a well-embedded knowledge management culture.

Note

1. Quoted in Mohr, J.J., Sengupta, S. and Slater, S. (2009) *Marketing of High-Technology Products and Innovations*. Published by Jakki Mohr. ISBN 0136049966.

8

Case study from British Telecom: supporting a distributed sales force

John Davies (BT), Ian Thurlow (BT) and Paul Warren (Eurescom)

British Telecom (BT) is one of the world's leading providers of communications solutions and services, operating in 170 countries around the globe. BT's principal activities include networked IT services, local, national and international telecommunications services, and higher value broadband and Internet products and services. Servicing many customers in the fast-moving telecommunications industry requires a large and dispersed sales and support force, with excellent access to up-to-date knowledge and information. In this chapter, John Davies, Ian Thurlow and Paul Warren describe ongoing research to improve this access.

Introduction

This chapter is about using knowledge management tools to help people working directly with customers. In fact, our user community are not all salespeople; some are technical consultants and specialists, and others are managers. However, they are all concerned with presenting and selling products and services to customers, and with ensuring that those products and services provide satisfaction to the customer and help sustain a long-term relationship.

These users are part of BT Business, a division of BT that provides for the information and communication technology (ICT) needs of a wide range of businesses in the UK. They are distributed across the country. They spend a lot of time with customers, but when not with customers they usually work from home. Because of their geographical spread, getting them together to share experiences is rare, so that electronic knowledge-sharing becomes very important. Apart from the problem of sharing knowledge, they suffer from the problems of information overload common to most of us. Moreover, they spend a great deal of their time navigating informal processes. These are not processes formally defined by the organisation, but processes created by themselves and their colleagues, and often not written down. They need help in being guided through those processes and in being provided with the right information at each stage. They also need to share and to improve those processes.

The intuition behind our work was that meeting these three challenges of knowledge-sharing, coping with information overload and using informal processes are fundamental to improving productivity – not just of sales people but of everyone who deals with information. We are developing a set of tools and technologies to provide solutions to these challenges.

For knowledge-sharing we are using a Web 2.0 approach, i.e. one that is lightweight and user-friendly. However, we are merging this with more formal, and in some senses more powerful, technologies developed within the computer science community. In doing this, we are creating powerful yet user-friendly tools.

We believe that a key to coping with information overload is managing information according to its context, that is, to how it relates to the user's activities. We imagine that for a sales person, context would often be defined by the particular customer he or she is currently thinking about. When the user is concerned with a particular context (or customer) the information provided needs to be prioritised according to its relevance to that context.

Finally, our approach to process management is, on the one hand, to provide easy tools to help the user describe those processes, so that they can be shared and improved. On the other hand, we are experimenting with techniques for learning common process patterns, so that when a user repeats those patterns, he or she can be helped to complete the process without having to remember the detailed process steps. Software is also being developed to improve on existing processes, i.e. to make them more streamlined.

All this work is being carried out as part of the ACTIVE project.[1] ACTIVE is a collaborative European research project running from 1 March 2008 until 28 April 2011. The project has twelve partners from across Europe. The BT case study described here is one of three case studies in the project. The case studies have been designed to use the project's results to benefit real users, while at the same time validating those results with the users. The project partners are listed below and more information can be found on the project website. An overview of the project is given in Warren et al. (2009).

ACTIVE has a number of partner organisations. The ACTIVE case study partners are Accenture (*www.accenture.com*), BT (*www.bt.com*) and Cadence (*www.cadence.com*). The technical partners are European Microsoft Innovation Centre (*www.microsoft.com/emic*), iSOCO (*www.isoco.com*), Hermes SoftLab (*www.hermes-softlab.com*), Jozef Stefan Institute (*www.ijs.si*), Innsbruck University (*www.uibk.ac.at*) and Karlsruhe Institute of Technology (*www.kit.edu*). The partners responsible for validation are Forschungsinstitut für Rationalisierung (FIR) (*www.fir.rwth-aachen.de*), kea-pro (*www.keapro.net*) and Project Management Eurescom (*www.eurescom.eu*).

In the next section we describe our users' requirements as well as the techniques we used to understand those requirements. Each of the following three sections then describes how we are applying the three aspects of ACTIVE to help our users in their daily work. After this we describe the users' initial reaction to our approach. Finally, we talk about some next steps.

Understanding the users' requirements

We started our work at the beginning of ACTIVE in the spring of 2008 by talking to a sample of people whom we hoped would benefit from our approach.

When we talked to the senior managers, their needs were clear. First, proposals need to be with customers more quickly. The quicker a proposal gets to the customer, the higher the chance of closing the sale. This must not be at the expense of quality; the need is to rapidly generate high-quality proposals. This means reusing information from previous proposals, but it must be the right information. It also means putting the individual or team writing the proposal in touch with those who have the expertise to help – perhaps specialist expertise in a particular technology applicable to that proposal.

Second, customer-facing people needed to be helped to be more proactive in interacting with customers. Rather than waiting for a customer to present their requirements, they need to anticipate those requirements. One way to do that is by understanding how a solution for one customer could be applicable to another.

With the technical specialists themselves, our work was organised in three phases. First, we undertook interviews with a sample of our customer-facing specialists. This was followed by 'job shadowing' to really understand how they use current technology and what their problems were. To save time, because our users were spread across the UK, this job-shadowing was done remotely. We were able to observe the user's computer screen and hear his or her conversations from our own office. Apart from the saving in travelling time, this technique had the advantage that our presence was less intrusive than if we had been physically present in the same room as the user. Finally, we presented our ideas to some of this community to get their feedback.

This work confirmed the message that we were receiving from senior management: that finding and reusing information and getting hold of the right people to help are important to success. We also found that some of our users are frequently switching context. We confirmed that context for most equated to the customer currently under consideration. Besides customers, other contexts may be relevant, e.g. a context for 'administration'. Some of the people to whom we spoke asked for the ability to download to their laptop everything (as far as is realistic) held centrally about a particular customer (i.e. context) before going out to meet that customer. They also thought it would be valuable to take account of their context when searching for information, both within the organisation and on the Web. The sharing of contexts was also seen as valuable. If contexts can be shared, this supports knowledge-sharing.

When we talked to the senior managers about informal processes, they were concerned with the proposal-creation process with which many of their people were involved. Creating good-quality proposals rapidly is seen as a significant challenge. Steps in the process include locating previous similar proposals, identifying relevant information and key experts, and getting the proposal adequately reviewed. A big challenge is to ensure consistency across a large multi-authored document.

Web 2.0 for knowledge-sharing

Our approach to knowledge-sharing is based on Web 2.0, the essence of which is that the consumers and producers of information are one and the same. From Web 2.0 we have adopted the technique of user-tagging and the tool of the MediaWiki.

User tagging – from folksonomies to ontologies

Knowledge-and information-sharing has been recognised as a significant problem by many organisations for several decades. Formal systems have been developed in which people place information in a repository, and at the same time classifying the information against a pre-agreed schema to encourage easy retrieval. While useful, such systems can be time-consuming to use since they require knowledge of the schema.

In the world outside the organisation an easier approach to information-sharing has been enormously successful. The use of tags to create so-called 'folksonomies' or tag clouds has enabled the sharing of web pages (e.g. with *delicious*[2]) and photographs (e.g. with Flickr[3]). The same approach is now being adopted within organisations and there are also attempts to achieve a synergy of the formal and informal approaches (see Hayman 2007). In ACTIVE, we are achieving this synergy by using lightweight ontologies to describe knowledge. An ontology is a formal knowledge model and the use of ontologies has been developed by the artificial intelligence community. Ontologies are formally defined and hence allow not just the description of knowledge, but also reasoning about that knowledge. The use of this approach greatly enhances information retrieval. For more information about the use of ontologies in knowledge management, see Davies et al. (2005).

By restricting ourselves to lightweight, relatively simple ontologies we are combining the benefits of the formal and informal approaches. Lightweight ontologies do not enjoy the full descriptive power that more complex ontologies have. However, they are computationally simpler and they are adequate for our purposes. We are providing an easy-to-use editor to create and edit these lightweight ontologies. The editor is intuitive to use and all the detail of what an ontology is and how it is used is hidden from the user. Moreover, if the user just wants to tag, they are free to do so. The system will learn simple ontological structures from the way in which tags are created and used.

Figure 8.1 shows a user tagging a document. The user can create their own tag. The system also suggests some tags based on the content of the document and tags used by others for related documents. Users can search on these tags, on document content, or on both. Figure 8.2 shows this.

Figure 8.1 Tagging a document, the user can create a tag or accept a suggestion

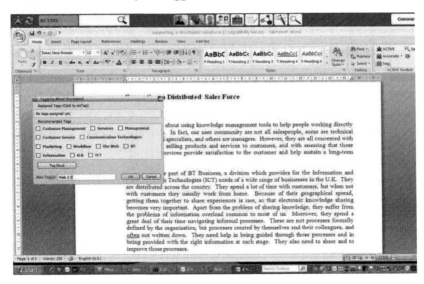

Figure 8.2 Users can search on tags or on content

There are a number of advantages to creating tags and searching on tags, rather than simply searching on content. A user is able to select as tags, words or phrases that are not in the document but that are particularly meaningful to that user and their colleagues. Even where a tag already exists in the document, the choice of this particular word or phrase as a tag gives it a particular significance that may aid document recovery. The use of recommended tags that have been used by others helps users converge on a common set of document descriptions, which creates an increased understanding of the relationship between documents.

Knowledge-sharing with the Semantic MediaWiki

As we have already observed, one area where sharing knowledge is particularly important is in creating proposals. Proposal writers need to find product information quickly and also appropriate text from previous proposals for reuse. The quality of proposals is also important. For example, where product information is used it must be the most up-to-date product information. A simple search on the intranet can often result in finding information that has been superseded. It is also important to find the right people who can contribute their expertise to developing the proposal.

Our solution to this is the use of a Semantic MediaWiki (Krötzsch et al., 2006). This is an extension of MediaWiki[4] that incorporates 'informal' semantics. In creating a link between two pages, authors may associate semantics with the link. In our example we will have a set of pages describing products, a set of pages describing technologies and a set of pages describing people. We can then, for example, have links from the people pages to the products and technologies in which they have expertise. We talk about 'informal' semantics because authors can make up their own relationships (e.g. 'is expert in') without reference to any predefined ontology. Of course, there is value in people using the same terms and they can be encouraged to reuse existing relationships; and it is possible to define equivalences between different terminologies (e.g. 'knows about' can be equated to 'is expert in').

Once such semantically annotated links exist they can be queried by the user, e.g. through a form-based interface. In our example above we can imagine querying the Semantic MediaWiki to provide information on everyone who is an expert in a particular technology or product. A query language can also be used to query the semantics to create HTML pages, for example a page listing technologies and the people who are experts in those technologies.

Where reference needs to be made to large documents, either a URL link can be used, for example to connect to the company intranet, or else a document can be uploaded to the wiki and made available from the appropriate page. In this way, documents, spreadsheets, multimedia objects, etc., can be accessed from the wiki.

The Semantic MediaWiki uses the capability of wiki technology to encourage collaboration. To have a community collaborating on text in a wiki is simply more effective than working with long e-mail threads. Moreover, the addition of semantic technology enables more powerful querying of the wiki than is possible with simple text search. It does this in a way that is informal and easy to use. Of course, text search is still available to complement the semantic features.

Delivering information in context

We have talked about the importance of being able to switch context easily, for example when a phone call or e-mail diverts us onto a different area of work. Figure 8.3 shows how a user can change context manually, by selecting a context from a drop-down menu. We are also using machine intelligence techniques to find out when the user has changed the focus of his or her work and thus when it would be appropriate for the system to switch context. This could be learned from the files they are accessing or the people with whom they are interacting via e-mail or instant messaging. While we believe some users will be happy to control their contexts manually, we feel the real value of our approach is realised with the use of these machine intelligence techniques.

Figure 8.4 shows how context can influence the delivery of information to the user. The user is opening a file within the word processor and specifying 'open in current context'. The five files shown are the most recently accessed files relating to the current context. Below this, the user is able to access files in other contexts. The user can also 'open' a file in the conventional way and see the most recent files irrespective of context.

Figure 8.3   User changes context

Figure 8.4   Opening a file in the current context

Understanding and improving processes

The third theme of our project is that of informal processes. Other researchers have observed the use of such processes by knowledge workers, in fact across a wide spectrum of professions (Hill et al., 2006). We similarly observed such informal processes amongst our users. These varied from relatively long processes, such as the creation of a proposal document that can take weeks, to relatively short processes that took minutes. Many of these short processes were to do with interoperating between different systems, e.g. copying and pasting from a spreadsheet to a CRM system.

As with the other aspects of work in ACTIVE, we are combining a top-down with a bottom-up approach. The former means we are providing a simple interface for people to create their own processes to be shared and reused. The bottom-up approach means we are using machine intelligence to learn processes and present these learned processes to the user for editing, sharing and reuse. The two approaches will, of course, be compatible. Specifically, learned processes will be editable through the same interface as is used to create processes top-down.

In fact, when we spoke to our users, their view was that generally they knew what step to take next but the issue for them was having the information they needed for that next step. So one aspect of our current work is designing a tool to present the user with the information objects they are most likely to need next.

The users' response

Before implementing our ideas we spoke to users to get initial feedback. Certainly our widely distributed users saw knowledge-sharing as a problem. Our users were familiar with the ideas of Web 2.0, although they generally did not participate in websites such as flickr that use tagging, nor did they contribute to wikis. Nevertheless, they saw tagging and the use of the Semantic MediaWiki as powerful ways to share information.

They also liked the idea of using context to deliver information, although as already noted, most felt that to obtain the real benefit from this requires the use of machine intelligence techniques to automate context detection and learning.

Turning to processes, the view of our users was that the real problem was not knowing the next step to take, but rather having the right information at each step in the process. Predicting what information is needed as the user works through a process is a key research goal for our project. We also found that people wanted to optimise their processes. As a first step to this, they wanted to understand what their actual processes are, as compared with what they are thought to be.

Next steps

As we write, our users are currently trialling the first prototype of our system. This will provide us with further feedback to inform our development activities. Later in 2010 we shall be trialling a more advanced system, with machine intelligence techniques for context detection and learning.

During 2010 we used the Semantic MediaWiki to assist knowledge-sharing, in particular for the preparation of customer proposals. When we talked to the people who prepare these proposals we were told that usually the core team writing a proposal could answer most of the questions posed by the customer in an invitation to tender. However, they would typically be left with half a dozen difficult technical questions for which they needed expert advice. Finding the right experts and getting that advice is frequently really difficult. The Semantic MediaWiki, with its semantic querying facilities, will help with information retrieval. One other feature we plan to incorporate is a publish facility, whereby those few questions for which there is no answer in the knowledge base will appear on the company intranet, inviting responses from across the company.

Perhaps the most ambitious of our features are to do with process learning and optimisation. These are still under development and will also be trialled later in 2010. The goal here is to really understand what our users' processes are and to streamline those processes.

The last six months of our project will involve extensive user validation. We hope this will further verify our intuitions. We also hope that this validation will enable us to improve our tools as a basis to encourage further take-up within and outside BT.

Acknowledgement

The work described in this chapter has been funded by the IST–2007–215040 EU project, ACTIVE.

Notes

1. *http://www.btplc.com/innovation/journal/BTTJ/current/HTMLArticles/ Volume26/26Improving/Default.aspx*
2. *http://delicious.com*
3. *http://www.flickr.com*
4. MediaWiki (*http://www.mediawiki.org*) is a free wiki software package, originally written to support Wikipedia.

References

Davies, J., Studer, R., Sure, Y. and Warren, P. (2005) 'Next generation knowledge management', *BT Technology Journal*, Vol. 23 No. 3, July. pp. 175–190. *http:// www.btplc.com/Innovation/Journal/BTTJ/archive/ArchiveHome.aspx.*

Hayman, S. (2007) 'Folksonomies and tagging', Ark Group Conference: Developing and Improving Classification Schemes, Sydney, Australia, June. *http://www.educationau.edu.au/jahia/webdav/site/myjahiasite/shared/papers/ arkhayman.pdf.*

Hill, C., Yates, R., Jones, C. and Kogan, S. (2006) 'Beyond predictable workflows: Enhancing productivity in artful business processes', *IBM Systems Journal*, Vol. 45, No. 4. *http://www.research.ibm.com/journal/sj/454/hill.html.*

Krötzsch, M., Vrandecic, D. and Völkel, M. (2006) 'Semantic MediaWiki', in Cruz, I., Decker, S., Allemang, D., Preist, C., Schwabe, D., Mika, P., Uschold, M. and Aroyo, L. (eds) Proceedings of the 5th International Semantic Web Conference (ISWC–06). Springer 2006.

Warren, P.W., Kings, N., Thurlow, I., Davies, J., Ruiz, C., Gómez-Pérez, J.M., Simperl, E., Bürger, T., Ermolayev, V., Tilly, M., Bösser, T. and Imtiaz, A. (2009) 'Improving knowledge worker productivity – the ACTIVE integrated approach', *BT Technology Journal*, Vol. 26, No. 2, February. *http://www.btplc .com/Innovation/Journal/BTTJ/BTTJHome.aspx.*

9

Case study from Mars, Inc.: knowledge management in sales and marketing

Linda Davies

Mars, Incorporated are a global company in the fast moving consumer goods industry, with six business segments including Chocolate, Petcare, Wrigley Gum and Confections, Food, Drinks and Symbioscience. These segments generate total annual revenues of $30 billion. As a family-owned company for nearly a century, Mars are guided by the five principles of quality, responsibility, mutuality, efficiency and freedom. The global reach of Mars' business segments and the inclusive nature of these values makes it important for Mars to learn, disseminate and apply knowledge and experiences from one market to another and between business segments. Additionally the fast-moving nature of the business requires a speed, immediacy and dynamism and therefore a fast, dynamic approach to sharing knowledge and expertise. This is particularly true in sales and marketing, where speed to market is of the essence. In this chapter, Linda Davies, Knowledge Management Director for Mars Information Services, explains how Mars use knowledge management within sales and marketing.

Introduction

Mars, Inc. use knowledge management (KM) throughout its business. For us KM is about the use of tacit information – the knowledge that our associates carry in their heads – as opposed to information that is written down and stored in databases. The type of KM and the tools used are the same throughout our business, but the focus and emphasis vary between the functions as a result of differences in the style and nature of the jobs and people involved. A key learning is to never pre-judge what will and will not work for a given function or community – keep an open mind, do not be afraid to try and be prepared to be pleasantly surprised!

For Mars, Inc., knowledge management is about developing and using what people *know*. It is about solving problems once and applying the results globally – piloting in one area for the benefit of all and combining the knowledge from a range of individuals to craft a solution to a new challenge. Above all it is about people and how to engage them in delivering results: What are we trying to achieve? Who knows what? Where and by whom can we actively apply this knowledge? The core KM team is thus focused on connection, collaboration and conversations – the essence of sharing, collaborating and applying knowledge.

We have standard rules for effective KM. Before we undertake any initiative we must be able to clearly articulate:

- Why are we doing this – what is the business benefit?
- What do we *need* to know (as opposed to what is nice to know) and how will this be used?
- Who has the knowledge and who needs it?
- What are their natural ways of working?

These questions determine the approach we take.

Toolkit

Mars, Inc. KM has three main components:

- the use of small, focused communities to address specific, well-defined, strategic business challenges, often with a short lifespan (maximum three years). In KM terms these are communities of purpose, although we know them as Global Practice Groups (GPGs);[1]
- the use of communities of practice to connect those with the same or similar roles – known either as communities or, increasingly, as networks;
- the use of formal knowledge-capture and dissemination for specific topics of global use.

These are supported and enabled by a comprehensive suite of IT tools.

Both GPGs and networks are types of community. The definition we use for a community (of any type) is 'a group of people with *common roles/activities* who share experiences, insights, knowledge and best practices in response to common challenges'. Or, more simply, 'people who share a passion for what they do'. The key lies in the common roles or activities. We have found that, to work, the focus of the community must be directly related to what an associate does in their day-to-day role. In this way it delivers value and saves time, which makes the time invested in sharing knowledge worthwhile.

Global Practice Groups

Mars use the concept of Global Practice Groups (GPGs) to address key strategic challenges. These are small groups of senior associates who are charged with delivering a step-change in performance in an area of strategic importance to Mars, Inc. Each GPG has a sponsor within the Mars Presidents' Group, a leader who directs, mentors, enthuses and enables the network and a coordinator who brokers the connections, provides a base level of resource and generally functions as the 'Energiser Bunny' of the group. The GPG members each has responsibility for the topic area in their business units and is sufficiently senior to be able to effect change. The communities have a specific, measurable challenge, a defined end target and the responsibility to deliver a step-change solution for the business as a whole. These are used in both marketing and sales, although have had more widespread use in sales.

For example, in our chocolate, gum and confections segments, a large portion of the sales are through impulse outlets.[2] In our newer markets in the developing world the bulk of consumer spending occurs in small local shops; the European/US model of large supermarkets has yet to take hold. It is critical to maximise the number of small retail outlets that sell our products in order to drive sales in these markets. To help meet this challenge, we have a 'Route to Mass Market' GPG, comprising the sales directors of our twelve largest new markets. Their markets are at varying stages of evolution and each member has unique areas of expertise and real success stories to share. No one director holds all the lessons; however, there are critical challenges running as a common thread across the markets and real bottom-line value is gained from sharing expertise and know-how. The GPG meets every six months, face to face, hosted by one of the markets. The meetings are focused on sharing, learning lessons and discussing. There are no formal presentations; numbers and details are covered outside the meetings. Instead, the meetings are based around three main activities designed to encourage the GPG to share its lessons and to build the knowledge base of successful processes and principles:

- learning from the market we are in (seeing things in action);
- learning from what we know (learning from the experience of others on specific hot topics);
- learning from the last six months' activities, often with markets piloting new ideas and approaches.

Communities of practice

Through trial and error we have learned the benefit of running fewer, large communities (with sub-communities as required) rather than having a multitude of small communities. This is linked to having a critical mass of people and hence multiple, varied activities and a wide range of ideas, expertise and knowledge available to members. In the early days there was concern about the relevance of broad-based communities. However, while at a practical level every job function and market is different and each has its own challenges, at a higher level many of the challenges are the same and the essence of what we are trying to achieve is the same. At this level, the basic ideas present in each job, function and market contain valuable lessons that can be adapted and evolved for others.

Hence our communities are largely global. At the centre is a steering team of senior, experienced associates who sets the agenda for the coming year and controls the centrally focused activities. Note that this does not preclude other activities occurring spontaneously throughout the year. However, it sets a regular pattern of activity, focused on important areas for the business, which ensures the communities make continual, relevant progress on core issues. In this way the community always has something new to offer its members, continuing to deliver relevant learnings to the members and value to the business.

Within each global community, there are sub-communities focused on particular topics. Each of these is led (championed) by a member of the steering group. These sub-communities are run in exactly the same way as the overall community, which provides the link for the sub-community to share its learnings with their colleagues throughout the business. These sub-communities deliver against interests and challenges associated with people's day-to-day jobs. In Marketing each community is focused on connecting the marketers who work on a specific brand – with six brands in excess of $1 billion each annually, this makes sense! However, we also have communities focused on specific aspects of marketing across brands – for example, establishing petcare in our developing markets. In general, our marketing communities are within product segments, since this is where the common themes lie. For sales, the communities tend to be focused on the type of sales job – for example, connecting associates who are responsible for sales to the grocery trade or the small impulse trade or selling through distributors. Hence in general our sales communities tend to cross the product segments. The common themes here are more likely to be related to the business model than to the product category.

A valuable addition to these communities, especially in marketing, is the inclusion of external partners such as advertising agencies. We have found that the wider the (relevant) membership of a community, the more value it generates. Hence the value of the community is enhanced by including our key partners.

Knowledge exchange

A key tool used by many of the communities, in both marketing and sales, is a knowledge exchange, which focuses on sharing what each member knows about a specific area. Known to the group as a 'show and tell', the topics are frequently fairly broad, since we do not always know what each other knows. To tightly specify a topic may mean a missed opportunity. These sessions take anything from half a day to two days (depending on the topic and number of attendees). They are focused on practical examples of solutions to a current hot topic. Prior to the meeting the community steering group identifies the topic. It may be a topic where a couple of markets are known to have expertise that the others need, it may be one where all have expertise and where there is interest in seeing the other good ideas, or where it is accepted that a more common approach would be beneficial. Each person at the 'show and tell' meeting has a 'display' in the room to exhibit the solution they are proudest of and a time slot to 'sell' this solution to the group as a whole. These solutions are always practical; it's a display, not a presentation. People are encouraged to bring objects that can be picked up, equipment for trial and photographs of examples in action. We have even built entire shop displays in hotel bedrooms! These sessions invariably create a huge amount of discussion and it is common for people to leave the meeting with samples from other markets to implement themselves when they get back home.

Formal knowledge-capture

Practical learning is immensely important for all functions and is the key to knowledge and information being used. However, formal capture also has a place, in order to develop a knowledge base to:

- share the learnings of this group with the wider audience in Mars, Inc.;
- ensure we do not forget what we have learned (especially when an activity happens relatively infrequently); and
- ensure our experts are not continually inundated with the same question.

Both marketing and sales have a programme of formal knowledge-capture with the results centrally stored, always electronically and often in printed form also. Each person who visits a website or picks up a booklet must learn something of value they can apply in their market. We distil knowledge and expertise down to the core lessons and word these as practical recommendations. The summary fits on one sheet of A4 paper. A good check is whether someone can immediately see how this would be applied in their market. A validation of the usefulness is then how many access the longer summary or visit the website for more information.

The community steering group identifies the topics that warrant formal knowledge-capture and identifies the experts. Formal capture is limited to strategic issues and areas of greatest learning, in order to keep it relevant, avoid information overload and focus scarce resources (knowledge-capture is time-intensive to complete). The learnings are captured through a series of interviews (individual or group), summarised into practical tips and recommendations and presented in three formats that support each other:

- a series of booklets containing top tips and advice;
- a website or wiki containing detailed information, templates, examples, etc.;
- a series of modular training courses.

The booklets and training courses are a valuable source of knowledge for those starting out or starting a new market. The website or wiki allows the community to update its knowledge base as it continues to evolve and to learn new lessons. Together they provide a comprehensive guide to each core area. These work in both sales and marketing with a different emphasis. The booklets are popular in both – sales makes greater use of the training courses and marketing makes greater use of the websites and wiki.

Go with the flow

The key to all our successful uses of knowledge management in all functions, not only in sales and marketing, is to match what we are trying to achieve with the natural style of the associates concerned. It is important to think what we are trying to achieve, what the associates need, where it will deliver value and, importantly, how they naturally work and therefore how they will access the knowledge and use it. We consider their working environment and their natural communication style; remember KM is about people talking to people! As a sweeping generalisation (and accepting there are notable exceptions), the preferred communication style of our sales people is the telephone, assuming they cannot get face to face. Therefore their greatest aid to connectivity is a simple expertise locator containing name, job title, location, phone number, e-mail and a photograph; it's easier to phone someone once you know what they look like! Marketing have made more use of technology, aided by being more likely at a desk and/or in front of a PC. Therefore websites and electronic connections work well for them.

We also take time to build activities into the normal ways of working. For example, whenever sales associates visit another market they will spend time visiting the stores, either as part of the meeting or on their own. Therefore a field visit is built into the agenda of each meeting of our sales communities and includes a KM activity. The 'host market' highlights their biggest successes and a couple of top challenges at the start of the visit and directs attention to examples of these during the time in the stores. Back in the meeting each group provides detailed feedback on what they see as working well in the market and how to build on the successes they see. They also give their top ten ideas on how to address the challenges, based on lessons and experience from their own markets. In this way the host market receives positive confirmation of their success and how to build on it, plus around thirty ideas and improvement suggestions targeted at their key challenges, based on lessons from proven, practical experience elsewhere in the world. Each member also nominates the one idea they saw during the day that they plan to adapt and implement in their own home markets. This builds realisation that everyone can learn from every experience and encourages the rapid adoption of new ideas. We have many examples of ideas from one market being replicated globally. Some ideas have travelled halfway around the globe and been implemented in a matter of months.

Technology – the great enabler

Technology is the great enabler for knowledge management. Both sales and marketing use a central website for core documents, news, etc. However, marketing uses technology more intensively, with systems for sharing advertising, packaging, brand images and other items. There is no difference in the rules; keep it simple, keep it relevant to my job, keep it refreshed and new, keep it vibrant and fun. It can be a challenge to establish the habit of using central technological solutions. In the early days we had to be fairly directive, making it the only place where certain important information could be found, continually directing people to it and resisting the temptation to e-mail information to people. Once a critical mass of users developed, the benefits sold the systems.

Summary

Overall there are a number of conclusions we can draw about knowledge-sharing in a global organisation such as this:

1. Focus KM on the important areas – keep all activities relevant and know how your KM activities will deliver business benefit.

2. It is important to get the network into a rhythm of learning and knowledge-sharing if it is to become second nature to the people involved.

3. For the key connection points, have regular meetings, face to face where possible, since the social interactions are key to building the level of trust required.

4. Keep the discussions, meetings and new knowledge shared focused and relevant to the members so they get real personal benefit from the sharing sessions.

5. In the early days, seed and nurture both the contributors and the knowledge shared. Your early adopters are critical, as is the initial content.

6. Keep it practical, so it is obvious to see how to apply what has been learned.

7. Get people to say how they have used the lessons and ideas and what the impact has been. This encourages people to take time to seek out and use the knowledge of others, encourages those who take the time to share their lessons with others and confirms the behaviour we are seeking.

8. Don't be too prescriptive – use what works for the community members.

9. Celebrate success and by doing so recognise and reward both lesson seekers and lesson sharers.

Notes

1. See Chapter 4.
2. A shop or stall where customers buy confectionery 'on impulse', rather than as part of a planned shopping list.

Case study from Ordnance Survey: social networking and the transfer of knowledge within supply chain management

Graeme Smith, Southampton Solent University

As Great Britain's national mapping agency, Ordnance Survey® is responsible for the maintenance of Great Britain's national map archive. It is widely regarded as a world leader in the production, maintenance and marketing of a wide range of maps and topographic data products for commercial business, leisure, education and public sector administration. OS MasterMap® lies at the heart of Ordnance Survey's business strategy; it is a massive database and online service. It includes data that is delivered online in themes such as roads, buildings, address data and imagery. Customers can also access change-only updates, cutting down the amount of data they have to manage. OS MasterMap is updated on a daily basis by field surveyors using hand-held computers to survey and digitise ground information. Map data files of the survey area are called down from the central database on to the hand-held computers and changes are made on the spot. This revised data is sent back to the main Southampton database and processed overnight so the new information can be accessed by customers the day after surveying.

The following chapter was written by Graeme C.M. Smith, Associate Lecturer in Marketing, Southampton Solent University. Graeme had responsibility for the development of the sales and marketing balanced scorecard that defines group performance; the development of strategy performance monitors; and the introduction of customer experience management at corporate level. Graeme has 15 years' experience in business process improvement in the sales and marketing environment serving customers across the public and private sector, either directly or through third parties in both commercial and consumer markets.

Introduction

For the purpose of this chapter, supply chain management is the process of planning, implementing and controlling the operations as efficiently as possible within the sales and marketing environment. The supply chain spans the tracking of all transactions from the identification of prospective customers, through quote to order conversion, fulfilment and on to post-sales support. As an intensive human activity, customer supply chains are wholly dependent on knowledge and require social network activity to transfer that knowledge to the point of need in order to reduce process variation.

This chapter builds upon work undertaken previously by the author, who developed an organisational model of the social interactions affecting knowledge transfer within organisations (Smith et al., 2003). This chapter also discusses the problems of knowledge location, the ability (as well as willingness) to share, the prevention of knowledge attrition through a programme of knowledge definition (codification), knowledge retention and knowledge transfer across the customer interface.

The argument is made that while much information is being shared, the knowledge that makes such information useful must also be transferred, or else new desired outcomes will not emerge. In order to share such knowledge, lessons were learned from three major studies that were carried out in 2004, 2006 and 2007 to determine the extent of failure to transfer knowledge within the sales and marketing supply chain at Ordnance Survey.

As a result of these studies, a programme of work was introduced to identify knowledge silos acting as centres of excellence in the supply chain and putting in place a project to preserve and transfer knowledge from these silos to facilitate learning and reduce knowledge attrition.

This chapter focuses on empirical evidence from these studies and the impact that this knowledge management project has had on the efficacy of the supply chain to deliver the desired outcomes.

For the purposes of this chapter, the focus is on customer orientation, the interface across the customer/supplier dyad and the transfer of knowledge through people, processes and systems. The methods of business process improvement as a means of changing culture are also reviewed. The overall aim of this chapter is to discuss the role of social networks in the successful sharing of knowledge within organisations.

What was the problem?

Sales and marketing management knew for some time that account managers and order processing staff were being distracted from the real focus of their roles and responsibilities towards dealing with growing customer demand that was the result of process non-conformance within the customer supply chain. At the same time there were a number of widely held assumptions regarding the nature of non-conformance and what was needed to reduce it. However, senior management was persuaded that a new way of thinking was needed to address the complexity of the problem. This new approach would consider the application of systemic thinking for human systems and processes, the methods of creating, organising and using information, and the transfer and application of knowledge. Internalising this systems view and the consequential impact on social networks should, it was felt, lead to practical and effective systemic action and process improvement.

Silos

There was growing anecdotal evidence that each iteration of management restructuring was driving knowledge into silos throughout the customer interface. There was also evidence that individual 'experts' were acting as knowledge hubs and exerting undue influence on the efficacy of the supply chain.

Enterprise-wide technical and management systems are needed for the efficient sharing and dissemination of information. However, creating these processes is not in itself enough to set the process in motion, since there are a number of individual and cultural barriers to sharing information. These barriers may coincide with functional or hierarchical barriers that can lead to the splintering of organisational information and its acquisition and dissemination, and management structures sometimes do not facilitate the collection and dissemination of information. Management and organisational culture has a large part to play in eliminating these barriers and the difficulty in reversing this process should not be underestimated (Probst et al., 1999).

Assumptions

Assumption 1: System implementation changes processes and behaviour

From discussions within sales and marketing it was clear that senior management felt that by changing the work processes within the organisation as part of an IT solution to facilitate a sharing of knowledge, new behaviours would emerge as a direct result. Thus the new knowledge that was accessible to all would encourage learning and new behaviour.

Assumption 2: Systems are mechanistic in nature

In discussions with employees (especially managers), there was a mechanistic view of the organisation as a machine, with the employees as cogs working within it. The focus within the company upon business process re-engineering and the way it is described supports this view of the organisation as a machine that can be rebuilt, fixed and have new parts fitted.

McAdam and McCreedy (1999) indicate that many knowledge management models reflect this old managerial paradigm and do not recognise the importance of the individual within the system (see Figure 10.1, where black arrows indicate expected behaviour and white arrows represent actual behaviour).

Figure 10.1 Demarest's knowledge management model

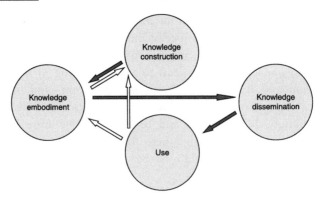

Demerest 1997

Assumption 3: Organisational systems will be rational

Operational managers within the Ordnance Survey knew that there were key processes within the system that were increasingly reliant on 'experts' in the back office and that these experts were being used by front-office staff such as account managers to help them resolve customer issues. This flow of knowledge from the front to back office was increasingly beginning to impact on the workload of these experts and their immediate workplace colleagues. This raised a number of concerns for senior managers, such as: where was this demand coming from, what was the root cause and what knowledge in the back office was being valued and exploited by the front office? McAdam and McCreedy (1999) go on to show that to ignore the social nature of knowledge development is to oversimplify the behaviour and to underestimate what needs to be done to develop knowledge management systems. Figure 10.2 shows this increased level of complexity.

It was logical, therefore, that if there is to be the requisite organisational learning required to develop new behaviours, there must be recognition of the constructed nature of knowledge within the new system.

Figure 10.2 McAdam and McCreedy's knowledge management model

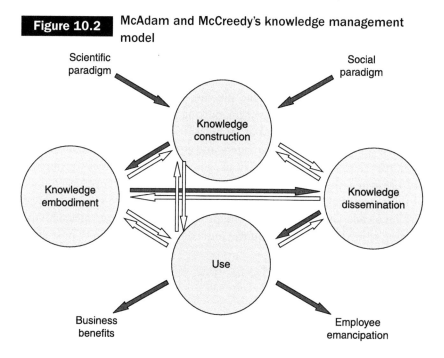

McAdam and McCreedy 1999

Methodology

Determining knowledge transfer within the process

There was a growing realisation within the business that in order to change the culture from rigid command and control to a more customer-orientated culture required a completely new approach. To determine this system view of the customer interface Ordnance Survey set up a small team of business analysts (service improvement team) who specialised in systems thinking and process engineering. The objective of the team was to define the sales pipeline (supply chain) that provided value to the customer.

The service improvement team facilitated a series of workshops with staff over a three-month period to codify processes (see Figure 10.3), business rules and local work instructions. To provide structure, prioritise work and feedback outputs from the workshops through to the systems architects, the service improvement team defined the sales pipeline as a logical series of steps through which customers travel in order to obtain data products or licences.

This new end-to-end view helped staff to understand better the activities they were responsible for and the part they played in adding customer value. The sales pipeline was then defined as seven key stages that would help to define particular process problems (see Figure 10.4).

The identification stage of the pipeline includes the identification of new markets, new prospects within existing markets and the production of marketing collateral aimed at stimulating market growth. New leads are then qualified by sales managers and pre-sales technical consultants and, for those that are passed as genuine opportunities, proposals are presented through negotiations with the clients. Once acceptance of these proposals had been reached, an order would be raised, fulfilled and invoiced. The final stage of the process involved post-sales activity, ranging from dealing with enquiries and complaints through to post-sales technical consultancy.

Demand audit

Having defined the people, process and IT systems extant within the sales pipeline, the next objective was to audit volume within the pipeline in

Figure 10.3 Process map showing hand-offs between teams and individuals

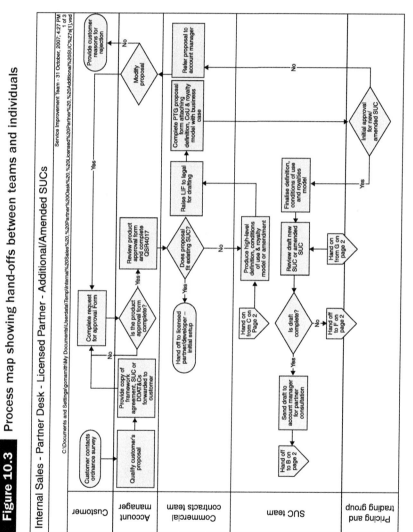

Internal Sales - Partner Desk - Licensed Partner - Additional/Amended SUCs

Figure 10.4 The sales pipeline

Demand generation			Service		Support	
Identification	**Qualification**	**Proposal**	**Acceptance**	**Fulfilment**	**Invoice**	**Post-sales**
Demand generation through planned and sustained market segmentation, research and communication; leading to product and service development to meet changing market needs. Defined within the scope of the overall corporate strategy.	Pre-sales activity forecasting and researching specific requirements for markets and customers identified as potential targets from our demand generation processes.	Specific product and licensing quotes defined by current business rules; pricing model; and contractual T&Cs.	Signed T&Cs and valid orders for processing.	Order processing and packaging, bill ship to; ship to customer, courier details.	Complete invoice details of licence; product details; customer holdings; and bill to details.	Provision of technical support to help customers develop added value from our products and services. Identifying sales leads and opportunities and passing them back into the sales pipeline.

terms of customer demand and the amount of human resource required to manage this demand. The scope of the audits was the whole of sales and marketing and included teams outside of sales and marketing, such as credit control (finance) and data supply (product management), which managed key stages in the end-to-end process. To date there have been three audits – 2004, 2006 and 2007 – covering some 200 staff.

Staff were asked to record time for a calendar month against a list of activities within the sales pipeline. Resource was measured in terms of hours spent serving the customer and getting it right first time (value add), as well as the amount of effort required to rework activity for the customer as non-conformance (process failure) – in other words process variation from the process standards set. The hours recorded by each member of staff were converted to salary cost plus expenditure and then annualised to provide the total annual costs of all staff involved in the audits.

Findings – 2004 audit

The study population included some 200 staff responsible for delivering marketing collateral, account management, customer service and pre- and post-sales activity. The response rate was 90 per cent.

Demand audit output

At the end of the audit the data were aggregated, analysed and profiled against the sales pipeline. This method of statistical analysis was delivered back to the teams involved and assumptions on the results clearly stated. Staff were then asked to participate in workshops to verify the data results and challenge the assumptions made. Initial workshops were process-based, including staff from various teams across the supply chain. A second series of workshops was conducted on a team-by-team basis. The reason for this was to try and capture the root cause of non-conformance from the process perspective and the business (team) perspective. This resulted in a more balanced view of the root cause of failure and each workshop acted as a 'sanity check' on the quantitative and qualitative data collected so far. The data analysis and workshop output were then presented to the senior management board to gain buy-in on the findings, conclusions, recommendations and the action plan required to prioritise and address process non-conformance.

The first audit took place in July 2004. Results were analysed through August and September, with the results and recommendations presented to the senior management board in October.

The 2004 audit presented a number of challenges to the senior management and service improvement teams. First, the volume of data and its comprehensive nature required an agreed structure (the sales pipeline) to analyse and report the audit findings. Second, there was the scale and complexity of non-conformance. Nobody had hitherto been able to present such a comprehensive picture regarding failure in both social network activity and IT systems. And third, there was the need to gain consensus and agreement on the data findings and to agree a programme to prioritise work for improving the customer experience. To address these challenges, the audit data was rigorously analysed and the findings aligned to the sales pipeline framework. This view made it easier to communicate the findings back to participants in a process view that they could easily recognise and understand.

The results confirmed management's view that account managers were spending too much time on post-sales activity rather than stimulating sales and new business. The audit results also gave management a great deal of detail on this resource imbalance, as the construct of the audit and subsequent data analysis brought into sharp relief the process activity that lay at the root cause of generating process non-conformance. The 2004 audit identified £1.05 million of process non-conformance, which equated to 21 per cent of the total salary bill for sales and marketing activity. As a result of the 2004 audit, a programme of process and service improvement was recommended and accepted by the senior management team.

Implementation

The consensus view was that a lot of the issues raised by the audit were widely known. What had not been appreciated was the nature and extent to which these issues had an impact all the way up and down the sales pipeline and the attendant cost. It was this new perspective that galvanised management and staff alike to clearly articulate the root cause and put forward business cases for process and IT improvements, underpinned by the costs of non-conformance derived from the demand audit data.

Knowledge experts

One of the more surprising results was the high levels of failure demand that some members of staff were having to deal with. Some were facing levels of non-conformance that were as high as 80 per cent of their total effort employed. Closer inspection of the data and workplace analysis of activities measured, revealed the nature and extent of the role these individuals were playing within the social network.

The most revealing aspect of their role was the fact that the rest of the organisation was using them as knowledge experts. They were being exploited for their knowledge, the position they held in the value chain, their propensity to help others solve customer problems and, to a certain extent, by their own management, who left them alone simply because they 'got things done' and helped the team achieve their key performance indicators. As a result of staff movements and retirements, these individuals were having to deal with increased demand and were becoming a scarce resource and a growing risk to the business. Their own lack of capacity to create and innovate change in the process due to volume pressures was reducing their ability to transfer knowledge to others. Of immediate concern to management was the high degree of risk that this built into the process. Individuals leaving their role would see a collapse of the social network previously dependent upon their knowledge.

Knowledge transfer

To address the known risk of knowledge hubs, the service improvement team identified the key players within the various processes. A series of workshops were conducted to establish the extent of the expertise that these individuals had in order to define exactly the range of skills and competencies employed. At the same time social network analysis was used to map the knowledge 'footprint' of each knowledge hub and their area of influence across the business, as well as the input to and output from each knowledge hub (knowledge flow and volume). The human system was dealt with as a matter of priority in order to substantially reduce this risk. The business analysts completely remapped the processes around the knowledge hubs and identified the knowledge requirement at activity level as they went along. The process mapping was used to codify tacit knowledge for future transfer and define roles and responsibilities.

Process definition

Apart from the work previously done on a pricing and licensing model, there was almost a complete absence of any clearly defined end-to-end process. The most that existed within the sales pipeline were local work instructions at team and an individual level. The lack of clearly defined process maps showing process hand-offs between teams and individuals had a huge impact on the amount of resource that was not aligned to the sales pipeline, leading to high levels of failure demand. This lack of definition was a major source of discussion at subsequent workshops. The absence of process maps led to job creep, as individual responsibilities were allowed to grow at the expense of neighbouring roles and responsibilities. In some instances this led to job overlaps. These overlaps caused severe problems as staff were transferred on promotion or personal development or exited the business. Managers recruited to backfill these vacancies discovered, often too late, that the job description bore no relationship to the scope of the role the previous incumbent actually fulfilled. Additionally, subsequent recruitment created gaps in the process hand-off that took some time to fill due to unplanned training and job role reconciliation with neighbouring staff in the process.

Once the process mapping stage was complete, the knowledge gathered was rolled into a knowledge and learning programme (see Figure 10.5) to transfer knowledge, skills and competencies. Skills matrices were defined for each member of staff, first to measure individual capacity to fulfil the requirements of the role and, second, to monitor personal performance as a basis for establishing future training needs.

IT systems

The root cause of sales managers spending too much effort on post-sales activity rather than generating sales was finally identified. The audit reported the problem as one related to order processing and the clarity of invoicing. The quote-to-order conversion process was not as smooth as it should have been, due to a number of previous IT improvements having been de-scoped. The result was that manual workarounds in the order processing areas were allowing order errors to creep into the IT system. Subsequent invoices sent to customers with information based upon

Figure 10.5 Knowledge learning cycle: communication to staff on the structure of the knowledge and learning pack

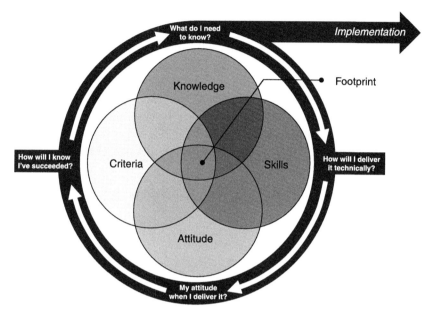

these orders were increasingly being queried by customers and sales managers were spending increasing amounts of time trying to resolve these queries. At the same time, call volumes in the contact centre were beginning to overwhelm service desk agents. Prior to the audit there were a number of stalled IT improvements and requests for change (RFC) that had been scheduled to resolve quote-to-order problems and invoice accuracy. These IT improvements attempted to automate the business rules that govern pricing and licensing.

As the Ordnance Survey is a licensing authority, these business rules are complex and not easily replicated in IT systems. The demand audit identified process and knowledge gaps where changing business rules had not been replicated through RFCs in the IT systems, as they were waiting for IT system architect resource. This meant staff having to create manual workarounds without necessarily codifying what these were. Additionally, RFCs had no cost metrics to help prioritise the work required to implement these changes. Process non-conformance costs from the demand audit were aligned to the RFC schedule to prioritise this work.

Findings – 2006 audit

As a consequence of the work done after the 2004 audit, it was decided to benchmark improvements with a second audit in 2006. The 2006 audit was structured along the same lines as the 2004 audit, with some improvements to clarify activity and to align results from both audits. The 2006 audit (Figure 10.6) showed that failure demand had fallen from 21 per cent of total cost in 2004 to 14 per cent in 2006. This was the equivalent of stripping out £0.4 million worth of process non-conformance on an annual basis. This released process capacity (£3.3 million, 46 per cent of total cost) to transfer resource to selling activity in the pre-sales part of the pipeline.

Figure 10.6 Total sales pipeline resource 2004–2006

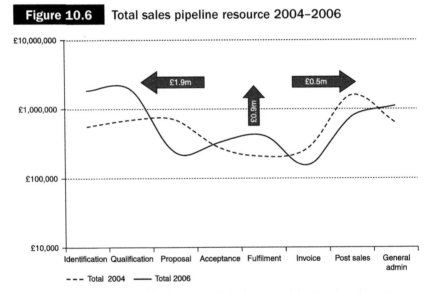

Note: The Y axis is on a logarithmic scale to help clarify the data; the data shows the annualised costs to serve through the sales pipeline

Total demand profile

The 2006 audit highlighted some significant movements in the demand profile. Further detailed analyses of the data at a team and individual level told us the direction and total value of this movement. Some of this movement was partly due to the elimination of non-conformance in the sales pipeline. It was this reduction that allowed senior management to realign resource towards demand generation in the pre-sales part of the pipeline. This movement could take place as a result of process improvements on proposal, invoice and post-sales activity, leading to a corresponding increase in identification, qualification and fulfilment (see Figure 10.6).

Total non-conformance profile

The cost of non-conformance fell by £0.4 million over an 18-month period between the two audits, the most significant reductions being in the proposal to post-sales parts of the sales pipeline (see Figure 10.7). These savings were largely due to facilitating the transfer of knowledge through the knowledge and learning programme (see Figure 10.5).

Figure 10.7 Total non-conformance 2004–2006

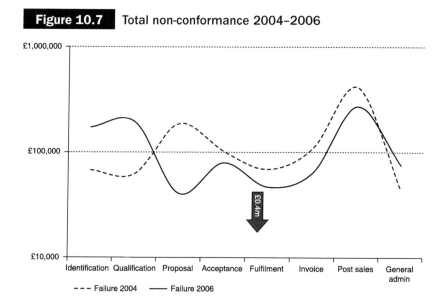

Team non-conformance

The impact of this reduction in non-conformance at a team level is illustrated in Figure 10.8. The data supply team is responsible for quote-to-order conversion of data requests and dispatching them to customers. The 2004 level of non-conformance was particularly high in the pre-sales part of the pipeline up to acceptance and in the post-sales part of the pipeline after fulfilment. The drop in non-conformance recorded in 2006

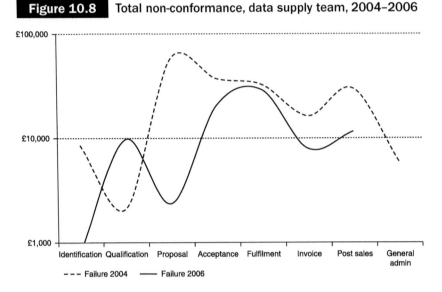

Figure 10.8 Total non-conformance, data supply team, 2004–2006

was due to process automation brought about by the results of the 2004 audit and to increasing the accuracy of order processing and that of invoices, leading to reducing the volume of customer enquiries.

The impact of this process improvement can be seen in Figure 10.9. This shows the total cost of resource employed by the data supply team

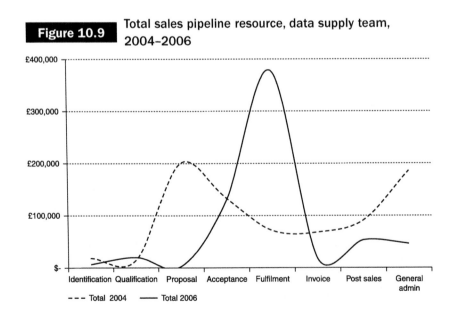

Figure 10.9 Total sales pipeline resource, data supply team, 2004–2006

along the sales pipeline and the realignment of team resource (worth £424,000) between the two audits.

Findings – 2007 audit

Concomitant to the realignment of the cost to serve in data supply shown in 2006 (see Figure 10.9), an additional £130,000 worth of resource was redeployed (Figure 10.10) to other parts of the business due to an overall drop in demand, driven by increased process efficiencies.

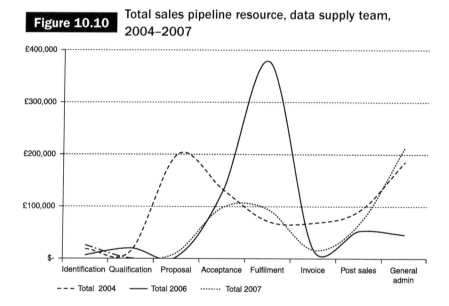

Figure 10.10 Total sales pipeline resource, data supply team, 2004–2007

Overall findings of the 2007 audit

The total number of respondents in 2007 was the same as that for 2006; 89 per cent of the population completed the 2007 audit. Over the three audits, non-conformance in 2006 fell by 35 per cent against the benchmark of 2004, and fell again by 34 per cent in 2007 against the previous audit in 2006.

Figure 10.11 shows a sustainable realignment of total resource in the sales pipeline. The effort in fulfilment dropped as a result of

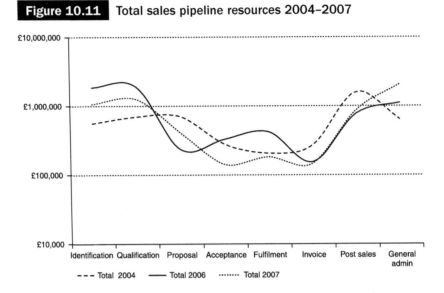

Figure 10.11 Total sales pipeline resources 2004–2007

continuing introduction of automation in order processing. Costs to serve are continuing to be maximised as resource in general administration continues to show an audit-by-audit rise over the three audits. This has had the effect of reducing overall cost to serve on account support activity, as support effort moves from high-value resource (sales managers) in terms of cost to low-level resource cost in administration. This is highlighted by the rise in demand generation activity (see Figure 10.4) between the 2006 and 2007 audits as sales staff start to increase activity in demand generation and post-sales support parts of the pipeline.

Was the problem due to ignoring social architecture?

It was the idea of social architecture affecting interpersonal relationships, structures, leadership, communication and, therefore, the successful passing on (or not) of knowledge that led to the publication of a series of papers from 2001 to 2003 and was of particular interest to the service improvement team. The work of the service improvement team established that the real challenge to knowledge transfer was one of communication. All communications models show filtering and 'background noise' as key elements in the success (or not) of the message and understanding transfer. By rethinking learning as being framed by the social architecture, it was seen that this background noise was acting as a filtering system. For example, emotions at work have always been acknowledged to have an impact but it is increasingly seen as having a serious effect on the efficiency of the outputs of any system (Clutterbuck and Megginson, 1999; Weisinger, 2000). They will always affect the potential receiver and will change over time.

Personal character traits

The degree with which staff are prepared to transfer knowledge depends on their dominant character trait at the time. The dominant character trait will depend upon the emotional state of the individual governed by current stimuli and/or past experience. The service improvement team found evidence that the rate and quality of knowledge transfer were being conditioned by personality and the environment that prevailed leading up to and between the first two audits. Between the first two demand audits of 2004 and 2006, the organisation conducted a staff opinion survey on a wide range of issues. Detailed workshops with a focus group from the customer service centre (some 35 per cent of the 2004 demand audit population) suggested staff were unwilling to participate in process creativity and innovation to improve service delivery. The main issues were management and leadership, lack of trust due to 'a blame culture' and the lack of defined boundaries between roles and responsibilities. Once these issues were seen by staff as being addressed, there was a noticeable improvement in the rate of creativity and innovation. Basically staff were simply 'keeping their heads down' until such time as a more enlightened management was in place and when they trusted the new regime.

Knowledge transfer

As the service improvement team began to close off remedial actions identified through demand audits, knowledge experts in the system and the lack of knowledge transfer, levels of non-conformance began to fall (see Figure 10.12).

Figure 10.12 Total non-conformance 2004–2007

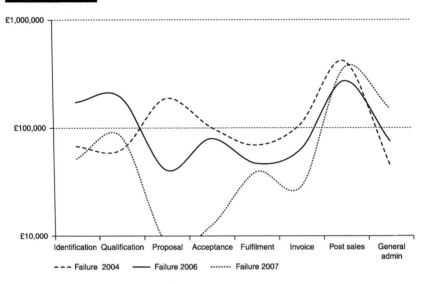

--- Failure 2004 ——— Failure 2006 ········ Failure 2007

The introduction of the knowledge and learning pack in 2006 (Figure 10.5) was designed to capture the tacit knowledge of the experts in the system and, through a programme of codifying and retraining, knowledge transfer could take place. Figure 10.13 highlights the impact that this programme had on the number of staff dealing with levels of non-conformance greater than 15 per cent of their total effort. In 2004 the total number of staff was 60; by 2006, 53 were dealing with less non-conformance – a drop of 88 per cent; in 2006 the number of staff

Figure 10.13 Reduction in non-conformance with knowledge experts 2004–2007

Pipeline	MU	2004 >=15%	2006	2006 >=15%	2007
Identification	Marcomms	–	–	6	5
Quote to order	PSU sales	12	11	6	6
	Partner sales	–	–	5	5
	Commercial sales	3	3	–	3
	Consumer sales	1	1	5	5
	Pricing & licensing	–	–	1	1
Invoice and fulfilment	CSC	28	22	30	18
	Digital supply	11	11	6	6
	Finance	5	5	2	2
Post sales support	PPSS	–	–	8	7
Total		60	53	69	58

was 69 and by 2007, 58 were dealing with reduced levels of non-conformance – a drop of 84 per cent.

Space

Creativity is not an event, it is a process. During the workshops between the first two audits it was an often expressed perception that staff did not have the time to change the way they do things. Some of the mapped processes were running to near capacity in relation to the number of people employed on them. There was a lack of 'thinking space' that negated staff's ability to be creative and to initiate change through successive approximations of the desired end result. It was soon realised that the service improvement team were in fact fulfilling this requirement.

Creativity involves a shift in the focus of attention and mode of thinking as we attend to what is working and what is not working. It can be individual or shared and can involve instant judgement or long-term testing. In most cases there are many shifts between these two modes of thought (Robinson, 2003). People don't have enough time to learn when processes are running to, or just above, capacity. An exclusive focus on efficiency can discourage learning. Managers who overemphasise results can subtly discourage technologies, skills or practices that make new approaches viable (Edmondson, 2008). In a customer service environment, staff have to have space to encourage the sharing of analysing insights, questions and problems.

Reward systems

Currently the organisation is implementing a new performance-related pay system based on behaviours, skills and competencies, which hopefully will act as a major incentive within the organisation. However, unless the employees see process key performance indicators directly relating to the new performance-related pay system, such a reward scheme will fail to support the successful implementation of new behaviour. At present there is no evidence that the new reward scheme will encourage process creativity and innovation. In fact, should reward be received without effective processes, as hoped, this will reconfirm old behaviours and make successful implementation of changes to process innovation even less likely.

Power

By definition, intentional networks have at their centre a knowledge hub actor who is a gatekeeper for the creation and transfer of knowledge. The focus of process demand on these players is predicated on their ability to expedite the creation, acquisition and transfer of knowledge required. This can create positions of power within the network, where the player may exercise a dominion over others in the network according to social conditions and personal character traits exerted at the time of exchange. Intentional networks are 'egocentric' networks that arise from individuals and their communication and workplace activity (Nardi et al., 2000).

These networks are personal. In contrast to communities of practice where workers inhabit a shared cultural space, intentional networks are the creation of individuals. Joint activity is accomplished by the assembling of sets of individuals derived from overlapping constellations of personal networks. These individuals have to create sufficient shared understanding to get work done, but such understanding must be collectively constructed rather than existing historically in an ongoing community or organisation. An intentional network is often much more distributed than a community of practice.[1] Workers are not thrown together in situation-dependent ways or assembled through outside forces. Instead, work activities are accomplished through the deliberate activation of workers' personal networks.

Conclusion

This chapter has shown that many knowledge management implementation problems are about the way the processes and systems for knowledge-creation are being developed in isolation from the social systems of the organisation. Rather than being a process problem, poor knowledge emergence from a new system is more likely to be a communication and learning problem, where there is a failure to engage with the individuals who are within the system.

However, at present many of these issues do not seem to be taken as seriously as they need to be within the organisations themselves. Organisations do not spend enough time diagnosing the root cause of failure to transfer knowledge within the process. Social networks exist for a reason, either to make an existing process work or, alternatively, to bypass the codified process due to failure in people who may be wedded to the security of known relationships and are refusing to change. Merely codifying the process as maps and local work instructions is vital but is nowhere near enough to anticipating entropy in the process as customer demand begins to drift away from the capability of a process to deliver the need of that demand. In many businesses it is this gap that increases in size due to management nescience as they focus on process output (by which time it is too late) rather than process input (knowledge transfer through social networks). It is this unconscious focus on outputs that costs organisations so much. By spending more time on organisational diagnosis of knowledge, how it is created and ultimately transferred (or not as the case may be), that benefit will accrue sooner, money will be saved and the pain outlined in this case study avoided.

Knowledge management caters to the critical issues of organisational adaptation, survival and competence in an increasingly discontinuous environment. Essentially, it embodies organisational processes that seek to maximise the combination of data and information processing capacity of information technologies and the creativity and innovation of the people who work in it. Up until now the maxim seems to have been that investment in new technology somehow results in improved business performance. Rather, managers should ask themselves whether success gained so far was due to an era of competitive advantage based upon the management of information as opposed to one based upon knowledge-creation in a learning organisation.

Enterprise-wide knowledge management systems are not a panacea for solving the problems of sharing knowledge in a company that aspires to be a learning organisation. Important though such systems are, it is the successful management of business processes as well as the cultural issues that relate to the way people are prepared and are able to share information that is of fundamental importance. The best practitioners have long realised that it is people that matter and that it is the human aspects of knowledge-creation that are critical for facilitating an enquiring mind and sustaining the learning organisation.

Note

1. The editors would not necessarily agree with this. There are plenty of communities of practice that have been created 'bottom–up' by the individuals concerned and are often extremely widely distributed. However, we would agree that the most effective communities extend beyond the purely personal networks.

References

Clutterbuck, D. and Megginson, D.(1999) 'Emotional intelligence in executive mentoring', Plenary Paper at 6th European Mentoring Conference, 25–26 November, Cambridge University.

Demarest, M. (1997) 'Understanding knowledge management', *Long Range Planning*, Vol. 30, No. 3. pp. 374–84.

Edmondson, A.(2008) 'The competitive imperative of learning', *Harvard Business Review*, July/August.

Goleman, D. (2006) *Social Intelligence*. London: Hutchison.

McAdam, R. and McCreedy, S.(1999) 'A critical review of knowledge management methods', *The Learning Organization*, Vol. 6, No.3, pp. 91–100.

Nardi, B., Whittaker, S. and Schwarz, H. (2000) 'It's not what you know, it's who you know: work in the information age', *First Monday*, Vol. 5, No. 5, May. *http://firstmonday.org/issues/issue5_5/nardi/index.html*.

Probst, G., Raub, S. and Ramhardt, K. (1999) *Managing Knowledge: Building blocks for success*. Chichester: Wiley.

Robinson, K. (2003) *Out of Our Minds – Learning to be creative*. Oxford: Capstone.

Russell, B. (1961) *History of Western Philosophy*. London: Routledge.

Smith, G., Blackman, D. and Good, B. (2003) 'Knowledge sharing and organisational learning facilitation through social architecture modeling', *Journal of Knowledge Management Practice*, 4. *http://www.tlainc.com/jkmpv4.htm*.

Weisinger, H.(2000) *Emotional Intelligence at Work*. San Francisco, CA: Jossey-Bass.

Setting up a knowledge management framework for sales, marketing and bidding

In the previous chapters, we have looked at some of the principles of knowledge management, we discussed some of the 'knowledge needs' involved in sales, in marketing and in bidding (and some aspects of the knowledge management frameworks to fulfil these needs) and highlighted a selection of the key knowledge management processes, technologies and roles that may be used in a sales, marketing or bidding context. Many of these were illustrated in Chapters 8, 9 and 10: the case studies from BT, Mars and the Ordnance Survey.

In this chapter we will help you through the thought process required to create a suitable knowledge management framework for your organisation and to 'pick and mix' the correct processes, technologies and roles for your context and business needs. We will present this thought process as a series of steps, with each step involving some decisions to be made and some questions to be answered.

Step 1: define the scope of your exercise

In other words, how much of your business do you want this knowledge management framework to cover? Given that the working styles of sales, marketing and bidding are so different and that their knowledge needs are so diverse, we would generally recommend that each of these disciplines has their own knowledge management framework. At a stretch, bidding and marketing could be combined, but sales will probably always need their own knowledge management framework. You may also need an additional knowledge management framework to cover the entire internal supply chain from product development to customer support, which will also cover elements of bidding, marketing and sales.

Step 2: identify the key areas of knowledge that people need

We could call these 'key knowledge areas'. These are the things that staff need to know in order to make correct decisions in their work. We have discussed some of these key knowledge areas in Chapter 2, ranging from knowledge of how to sell or how to construct an effective bid, through to knowledge of the client and knowledge of the product. Product and customer knowledge has traditionally been covered in various CRM and product databases and it is very often the 'how to' knowledge that needs more attention.

Step 3: for each knowledge area, define the source and user of the knowledge

The source of the knowledge is where the knowledge will originally come from. Almost always, this source is a person with experience or knowledge. So product knowledge initially comes from the product development team, customer knowledge comes from the people who interact with the customers, practice-related know-how comes from experienced practitioners. The user of the knowledge is the person who will apply that knowledge to make decisions or the person who will supply that knowledge to the customer. It is the marketing team, the bidding team, the customer-facing sales representative, who need to make knowledgeable decisions and informed recommendations. The purpose of the knowledge management framework is to provide an effective flow of knowledge from the source to the user, so that the user gets the information they need, in the format they need it, when they need to make the decision.

Step 4: define whether this knowledge can be transferred as tacit, explicit or both

Sometimes the knowledge can be transferred by conversation and through dialogue (for example, in an online discussion forum, through discussion as part of a team, through individual coaching and mentoring or through processes such as peer assist and knowledge exchange). This is possible when the source and the user are working in the same time zone or are otherwise available to each other, and when this type of knowledge transfer is relatively rare so that the conversational transfers do not become an unmanageable workload. Sometimes, however, it makes more sense to write the knowledge down, either because there are hundreds or thousands of users or because the knowledge needs to be transferred forward in time to future users who are not around at the moment to hold the dialogue. In this case, there needs to be some sort of capture of knowledge in a process document and knowledge asset, a portal or a wiki.

Step 5: if knowledge transfer is tacit, define the communication mechanism

Decide whether you need to set up a community of practice, a community of purpose or a community of interest. Work with the community to define the toolset that this community will use. Decide the processes that it will use, such as knowledge exchange, peer assists, 'show and tell', etc. Define the roles and accountabilities and appoint people as sponsor, leader, core team, facilitator – whatever roles may be required. Decide whether bid projects or marketing projects need peer assists with the other bid or marketing projects. Decide who is accountable for arranging and facilitating these peer assists. Decide whether you need the yellow pages technology to find the peers from around the world. Choose a set of technologies, processes, roles and community structures that will allow the most efficient and effective communication of knowledge between source and user.

Step 6: if knowledge transfer is explicit, define the capture mechanism

The first step in explicit transfer of knowledge is to make the knowledge explicit. Knowledge comes from people's experience and so needs to be captured and written down and done so in such a way as to retain as much value as possible. Define the processes you will use for this, whether you are using retrospect at the end of each bid, after action reviews during team meetings, individual submission of knowledge to a system or interviews of particularly knowledgeable personnel (or indeed a combination of processes). Decide who is accountable for making sure that these happen and happen well. Who quality-controls the process, for example? If the process doesn't happen, who should take responsibility for it not happening? Also, define the technology that you will use for capturing the knowledge, whether this is a database, a wiki, a collaboration system or documents on a file server.

Step 7: define the organisation method

Capturing knowledge is the first step; the knowledge then has to be organised, sorted and sifted to be useful and to be accessible. Wikis have to be edited and cross-linked, knowledge bases have to be sorted, common practices have to be turned into current best practices, documents such as the company marketing way have to be constructed. Define who is accountable for this. Who stewards and maintains the knowledge on behalf of the company? Who keeps it fresh? Who commissions the interviews and compiles the results? Define the technology where this knowledge will be stored and made available. Will it be a wiki? Will it be a portal? Will it be a push database, with RSS feeds and tabs? Define the processes for maintaining this knowledge. How often is it upgraded? How often is it reviewed? How do you reconcile differing opinions? How do you decide whether an innovation becomes the next best practice?

Step 8: define the distribution and internalisation mechanism

Even if captured knowledge is well organised and made available, it still needs to reach the user. The user must be able to find it, where and when they need it. You have to define how the knowledge will reach the user and what technology they will use to access it, depending on their work style. Are they sales reps, working with a customer, who need to be able to access knowledge from their smart phones? Are they members of a bid preparation team, working in an office with access to computers and laptops? Do they have search capability; do they browse on tags or use RSS feeds? Also, when should they be looking for the knowledge? At the start of projects or all the way through? Do they need to access the product database before every client engagement? Also, who is accountable for making sure people access the knowledge they need? The individual, the project leader, the sales manager? You need to think through all of these questions.

Step 9: define how you will measure knowledge management activity

How do you know whether people are using the knowledge management framework and using it well? Can you see who is contributing and who is accessing? Can you see knowledge being reused in subsequent bids? Do you have examples where successful marketing campaigns or successful product launches are reused in other parts of the world? Can you see customer service improving and sales and market share increasing? And if people are not contributing to knowledge management, are not sharing their knowledge or not reusing the knowledge of others, how would you be able to tell? If the processes and technologies and roles are not working, would you be able to see this? You need to define a means of tracking knowledge management activity so that you can intervene when necessary.

Step 10: define how you will manage the performance of knowledge management

Once you have decided how you will measure the performance of knowledge management, your final decision is how you will manage this performance. If people or teams are performing well, sharing their knowledge and reusing the knowledge of others, you need to decide how this will be fed through into their recognition and rewards. And if they are not performing well and refusing to fulfil their accountabilities and expectations in terms of knowledge management, you need to decide what will happen as a result. How can these people be encouraged to take part in knowledge management?

We cannot tell you how to make the decisions and answer all of the questions in the 10 steps above. However, in this book we have given you a range of processes, technologies and roles and a series of examples of how these have been used by bid teams, marketing teams and sales forces. It is now up to you to take these examples, roles, technologies and processes and create a knowledge management framework for your workforce, in your context, to address your business needs.

We wish you every success!

Appendix – customer buying process

The following flowcharts are intended as a checklist or prompt when reflecting on your knowledge management processes, roles and technology.

Figure A.1 is about recognising what your customers' needs might be.

Figure A.1 Needs recognition and problem awareness

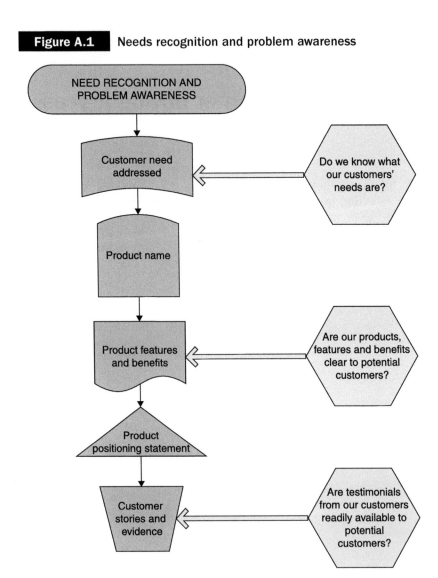

Figure A.2 is about your potential customers searching for information.

Figure A.2 Information search

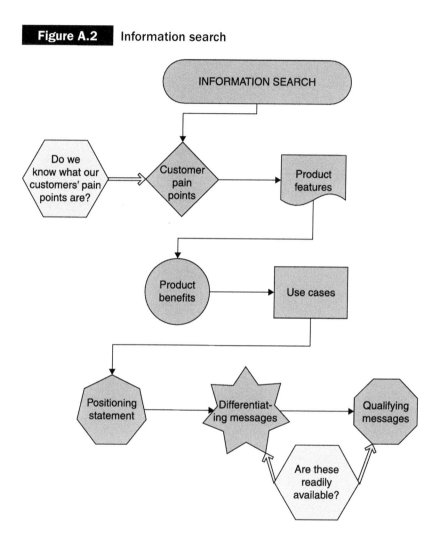

Figure A.3 is about how the potential customer may review potential alternatives to your principal offer.

Figure A.3   Alternatives

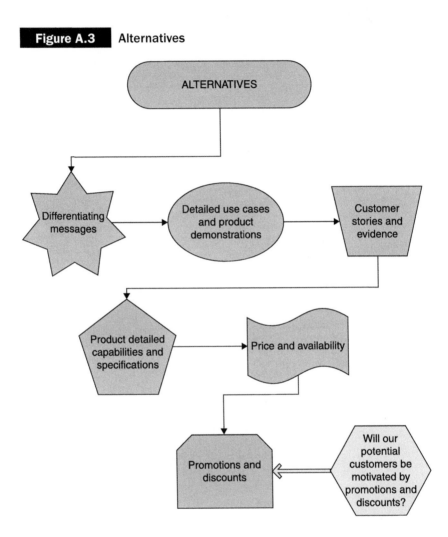

Figure A.4 is about the actual purchasing process itself.

Figure A.4 Purchase

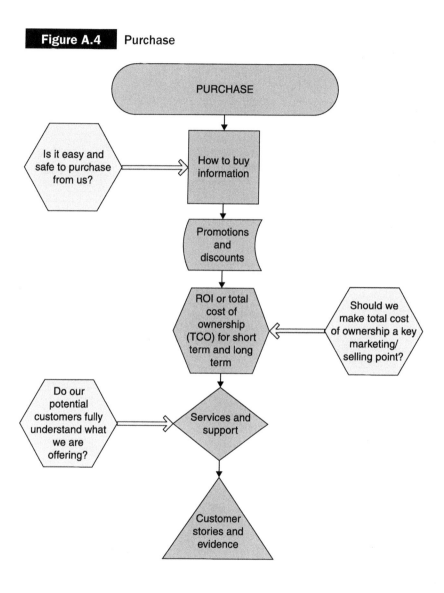

Figure A.5, the final checklist/flowchart, covers the post-purchase situation and the need to avoid a buyer remorse situation arising.

Figure A.5 Post-purchase evaluation

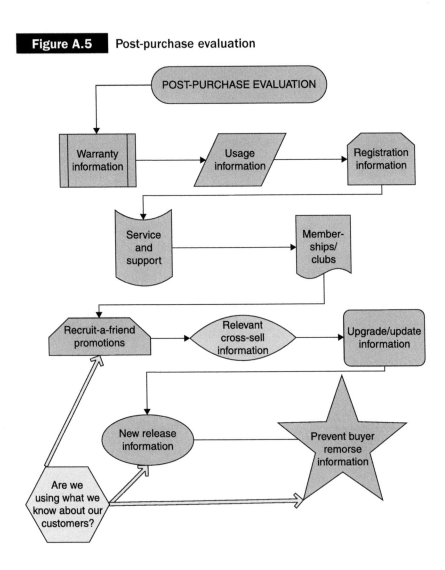

Index

Printed and bound by CPI Group (UK) Ltd, Croydon, CR0 4YY

08/05/2025

01864971-0002